COMPACT *Research*

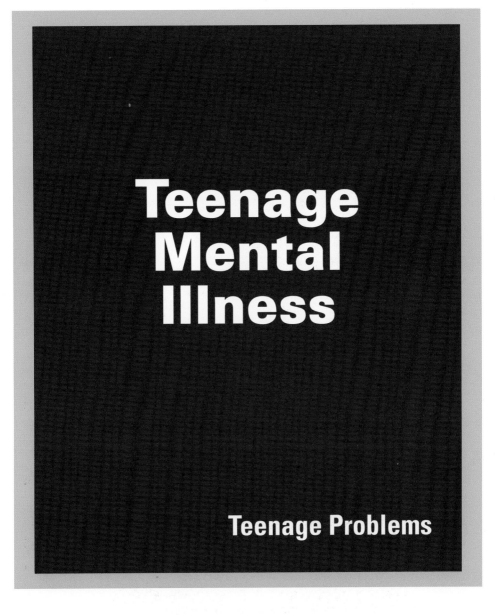
Teenage Mental Illness

Teenage Problems

ReferencePoint Press®

San Diego, CA

Other books in the Compact Research Teenage Problems set:

*For a complete list of titles please visit www.referencepointpress.com.

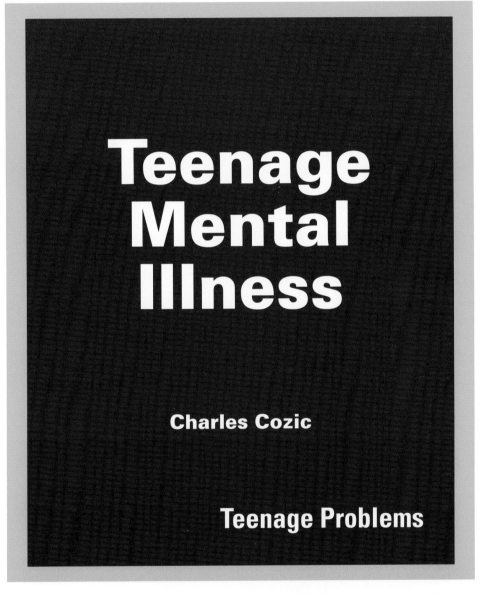

Teenage Mental Illness

Charles Cozic

Teenage Problems

ReferencePoint
Press®

San Diego, CA

© 2012 ReferencePoint Press, Inc.
Printed in the United States

For more information, contact:
ReferencePoint Press, Inc.
PO Box 27779
San Diego, CA 92198
www.ReferencePointPress.com

Picture credits:
Cover: iStockphoto.com and Thinkstock/Comstock
Maury Aaseng: 33–35, 47–49, 61–63, 75–77
AP Images: 15
© Ocean/Corbis: 19

LIBRARY OF CONGRESS CATALOGING-IN-PUBLICATION DATA

Cozic, Charles P., 1957–
Teenage mental illness / by Charles Cozic.
p. cm. — (Compact research)
Includes bibliographical references and index.
ISBN-13: 978-1-60152-167-5 (hardback)
ISBN-10: 1-60152-167-7 (hardback)
1. Teenagers—Mental health—Popular works. 2. Adolescent psychology—Popular works.
I. Title.
RJ499.34.C69   2011
616.8900835—dc22

2011012465

Contents

Foreword

"Where is the knowledge we have lost in information?"

—T.S. Eliot, "The Rock."

As modern civilization continues to evolve, its ability to create, store, distribute, and access information expands exponentially. The explosion of information from all media continues to increase at a phenomenal rate. By 2020 some experts predict the worldwide information base will double every 73 days. While access to diverse sources of information and perspectives is paramount to any democratic society, information alone cannot help people gain knowledge and understanding. Information must be organized and presented clearly and succinctly in order to be understood. The challenge in the digital age becomes not the creation of information, but how best to sort, organize, enhance, and present information.

ReferencePoint Press developed the *Compact Research* series with this challenge of the information age in mind. More than any other subject area today, researching current issues can yield vast, diverse, and unqualified information that can be intimidating and overwhelming for even the most advanced and motivated researcher. The *Compact Research* series offers a compact, relevant, intelligent, and conveniently organized collection of information covering a variety of current topics ranging from illegal immigration and deforestation to diseases such as anorexia and meningitis.

The series focuses on three types of information: objective single-author narratives, opinion-based primary source quotations, and facts and statistics. The clearly written objective narratives provide context and reliable background information. Primary source quotes are carefully selected and cited, exposing the reader to differing points of view. And facts and statistics sections aid the reader in evaluating perspectives. Presenting these key types of information creates a richer, more balanced learning experience.

For better understanding and convenience, the series enhances information by organizing it into narrower topics and adding design features that make it easy for a reader to identify desired content. For example, in *Compact Research: Illegal Immigration*, a chapter covering the economic impact of illegal immigration has an objective narrative explaining the various ways the economy is impacted, a balanced section of numerous primary source quotes on the topic, followed by facts and full-color illustrations to encourage evaluation of contrasting perspectives.

The ancient Roman philosopher Lucius Annaeus Seneca wrote, "It is quality rather than quantity that matters." More than just a collection of content, the *Compact Research* series is simply committed to creating, finding, organizing, and presenting the most relevant and appropriate amount of information on a current topic in a user-friendly style that invites, intrigues, and fosters understanding.

Teenage Mental Illness at a Glance

Impaired Function

Mental illness affects the thinking, concentration, mood, behavior, and/or perception of adolescents. These disorders impair one or more areas of functioning related to school, work, or social and family interactions.

Common Mental Illnesses in Teens

The mental illnesses that most commonly affect teenagers are depression, ADHD, and bipolar disorder.

Prevalence

Mental illnesses can strike any teenager regardless of his or her background or intelligence. An estimated 20 percent of American teenagers—approximately 4 million—suffer from a diagnosable mental illness at some point during adolescence.

Causes and Risk Factors

Experts have been unable to pinpoint a specific cause for mental illness in teenagers. Risk factors include inheriting specific genes from parents that make a child susceptible to mental disorders, other medical conditions, family environment, and life events.

Signs and Symptoms

Teenage mental illnesses are marked by symptoms such as sadness, hopelessness, aggression, restlessness, difficulty concentrating, lack of enthusiasm, extreme fear or worry, and thoughts of death. Warning signs may be difficult to recognize or may be mistaken for a different problem.

Common Problems

Adolescents who suffer from mental disorders face problems ranging from poor schoolwork to abuse of alcohol or drugs to thinking about suicide. These problems can become very serious if mental illnesses are left untreated.

Types of Treatment

The majority of teenagers treated for a mental illness receive a combination of psychiatric therapy and prescribed medication.

Medication

Medications are designed to treat the symptoms of mental disorders and make teenagers feel better, but they cannot cure the illness. Some medications also have serious side effects.

The Future

Researchers are studying the relationship between mental disorders and the brain. Some of these studies focus on how the teenage brain grows.

Overview

"About 20 percent of U.S. youth during their lifetime are affected by some type of mental disorder to an extent that they have difficulty functioning."

—National Institute of Mental Health, a federal government agency.

Less than a century ago few people had ever heard of the term *child psychiatry*, a field of study then in its infancy. At that time, few schools and institutions specifically for mentally ill children existed, but they were slowly increasing in number. Social reformers, educators, legislators, and others recognized a need to improve the care of mentally ill children. Aside from cases of severe mental retardation, these advocates could only guess as to what actually caused some children to suffer from other mental disorders such as depression and schizophrenia. Some experts theorized that such illnesses were the result of childhood head injuries. Others maintained that mental illnesses might be inherited from a parent, or perhaps even be associated with moral weakness.

As the study and practice of child psychiatry increased, so too did the number of theories about childhood mental illnesses. For example, many early child psychiatrists discounted the notion that children or adolescents could fall victim to the type of depression, anxiety, and other mental disorders that plagued adults. According to British child psychiatrist Richard Harrington, "Until the 1970s it was believed that depressive disorders resembling adult depression were uncommon among the young."[1] Many experts theorized that children's still-maturing brains lacked the necessary psychological components to be truly affected by a mental disorder.

Others who evaluated children with serious psychological problems deemed that parental behavior was largely responsible for their condition. In the 1940s and 1950s, for example, noted psychiatrists—including Theodore Lidz and Frieda Fromm-Reichmann—theorized that domineering, weak-willed, or emotionally distant parents played a key role in children's autism, schizophrenia, and similar disorders. Referring to Fromm-Reichmann, clinical psychologist Neil Frude wrote, "It is greatly to be regretted that her ideas once had a profound influence on clinicians, for this account essentially blamed mothers for their sons' and daughters' suffering."[2] Over time this type of theory lost prominence as alternative theories suggesting various genetic, biological, and environmental causes gained acceptance. Today the consensus among mental health experts is that adolescent mental illnesses are complex conditions that are as serious a threat to young people as cancer, diabetes, sexually transmitted diseases, and other physical illnesses.

> A mental illness is a disorder that impairs or interferes with a person's ability to function effectively in order to learn, communicate, or work.

What Is Teenage Mental Illness?

A mental illness is a disorder that impairs or interferes with a person's ability to function effectively in order to learn, communicate, or work. These disorders can affect people of all ages, from very young children to the elderly. Human beings experience strong emotions such as sadness, joy, anger, and anxiety on a regular basis. These feelings can be described as the normal ups and downs of everyday life. In many cases, therefore, identifying a mental illness in a person as opposed to his or her temporary emotional state of mind is not an easy task. Doing so can be even more difficult when those involved are teenagers.

Like adults, teenagers vary in personality and temperament. Some are quiet and shy; others are socially outgoing or risk takers. Some may be wary and cautious, while others are impulsive and reckless. Adolescence can frequently be a period of turmoil, and many teens have trouble coping with the anxiety and stress that this stage of life brings. Beginning at puberty, boys' and girls' bodies and minds undergo rapid changes. Also, their personalities are still developing—along with their sexuality—up to and into adulthood. Many teens may easily be overwhelmed by these changes, struggling with moods and emotions they had never before experienced. They may routinely act moody or anxious as they become more independent, face peer pressure, and strive to keep up with the demands of school, work, and family.

> There are many different anxiety disorders that teens may suffer from, ranging from a reluctance to speak to sudden panic attacks.

For these reasons, it can be challenging for parents, teachers, counselors, and others to determine whether a youth is exhibiting typical teen behavior or is struggling with a mental disorder, of which there are dozens.

Types of Teenage Mental Illness

Mental illnesses affect 1 in 5 adolescents—or approximately 4 million teens—a large percentage of whom never receive any type of treatment for their disorders. Teenage mental illnesses may be classified into three categories: mood disorders, behavioral disorders, and anxiety disorders. The two main types of mood disorders are depression and bipolar disorder. Depression is perhaps the single most common mental disorder among teenagers—about 20 percent of teens have experienced depression at some point, including severe depression. This type of depression, known as clinical depression, goes beyond brief sadness or just having a bad day. It affects the whole person—the way one feels, thinks, and acts—and is characterized by feelings of sadness, hopelessness, pessimism, loss of interest in activities, and low energy. Severe depression may last for weeks, months, and even years, and it can cause serious problems such as failure in school, substance abuse, and suicide.

Similar to depression—and perhaps more confounding—is bipolar disorder. Those who suffer from bipolar disorder experience extreme mood swings, from the lows of depression to the opposite of the spectrum, known as mania. Symptoms of bipolar mania include a great increase in energy, talking too much or too fast, sleeplessness, and excessively risky behavior. Symptoms in adolescents may differ from those experienced by adults. For example, during what is known as a manic state, teens may tend to be irritable or prone to destructive outbursts, compared to adults, who tend to act extremely elated or euphoric.

Anxiety Disorders

Anxiety is a common sensation of worry or uneasiness that is felt when a person faces a stressful situation, physical danger, or threat. In these circumstances the human brain triggers a bodily response much like an alarm system: a quicker heartbeat, along with sweaty palms, tense muscles, or trembling hands and legs. Though entirely natural, anxiety can also become a mental disorder if it is prolonged enough or so severe that it impairs someone's normal functioning.

There are many different anxiety disorders that teens may suffer from, ranging from a reluctance to speak to sudden panic attacks. Collectively, anxiety disorders are the most common of mental illnesses affecting youths, who may worry excessively about issues such as grades or exams, relationships with peers, personal health or well-being, family matters, or performance in extracurricular activities. They may also feel very uncomfortable being in certain social situations such as speaking in public or being the center of attention. The buildup of anxiety often causes undue stress, impairing a youth's thinking and behavior.

Phobias and Panic Disorder

Phobias are persistent fears, such as fear of heights or fear of flying, that can affect people of all ages. Teenagers are susceptible to certain types of phobias, both mild and severe. One such phobia is social anxiety disorder, in which a person feels overwhelming self-consciousness or anxiety in everyday situations. A teen, for example, may have a deep fear of being watched or being around other people, which can cause sweating, trembling, and even nausea. A related disorder is selective mutism, marked by a youth's inability to speak in social situations such as in a crowd and especially in a classroom.

A more severe and debilitating fear-related illness is panic disorder (PD), marked by unpredictable and frequent panic attacks usually lasting for several minutes. Such attacks can leave teens feeling faint, struggling for breath, or even experiencing nausea or chest pain. Teens with panic disorder often have anxiety about future attacks. Known causes include high stress and traumatic events, but other causes might also exist. In the words of child psychologist Gayle Zieman: "Often PD begins with no identified stressful event. It is common for a child to have periods of time with attacks and then go weeks or months with few or none. What causes attacks to stop and return is often unclear."[3]

While anxiety disorders pertain to present or future events, one disorder is linked to past events: post-traumatic stress disorder (PTSD). Adolescents who suffer from this illness have experienced or witnessed a traumatic past event, perhaps as long ago as when they were young children. This event may have been the tragic death of someone close to them, being in a serious accident, experiencing violence, or being the victim of physical or emotional abuse. Teenagers with PTSD often re-experience the traumatic event through nightmares or flashbacks, a way of reliving the memory. These youths often experience depression, difficulty concentrating, emotional detachment, loss of interest or affection, irritability, aggression, and sleep problems. They may also try to avoid certain situations or places that remind them of past traumatic events.

Attention-Deficit/Hyperactivity Disorder

Almost as common as depression among teens is a behavioral disorder known as attention-deficit/hyperactivity disorder, or ADHD. This illness—which begins in childhood—is marked by symptoms that include difficulty staying focused and paying attention, difficulty controlling behavior, impulsiveness, restlessness, and hyperactivity (overactivity). It was previously thought that most children outgrew ADHD by the time they reached adolescence. However, studies have shown that ADHD is more common among teens than younger children. According to the American Academy of Pediatrics, "Research has shown that ADHD persists into adolescence and beyond for 70% to 85% of children diagnosed with the condition."[4] As with other teenage mental illnesses, youths with ADHD may also suffer simultaneously from other disorders such as depression or anxiety disorders.

A teacher and student work together on a class assignment. The ability to focus on class work and on a teacher's instructions eludes young people who struggle with mental illness.

What Causes Mental Illness in Teenagers?

Teenage mental illnesses are perplexing disorders, since experts cannot determine precisely why some teens suffer from them while others do not. Mental health professionals cite a combination of genetic, biological, and environmental factors. It may be likely, for example, that mental illness runs in families, with one or both parents having a mental illness, thus increasing the odds that their child will develop the same disorder. Environmental factors may also play a contributing role. For instance, a child growing up in a family or neighborhood atmosphere marked by dysfunction, conflict, or violence may have a higher risk of developing a mental disorder.

While genetic or environmental causes may be difficult to establish, experts seem to have a more thorough understanding of the biological aspects of teens' mental disorders. The human brain contains billions of specialized nerve cells (neurons) that communicate with each other with the help of various types of chemicals known as neurotransmitters. These powerful chemicals create and control signals both between and within neurons, thereby managing virtually all of our functions, such as physical movement, thought processes, emotional states, and response to pain. Those neurotransmitters that affect a person's behavior include serotonin, norepinephrine, and dopamine.

Researchers have determined that these neurotransmitters have great influence on mood and that too much or not enough of these chemicals may cause a variety of mental disorders. Studies have found that low levels of serotonin can lead to problems such as lack of focus, fatigue, and sleeplessness and can cause illnesses such as depression, anxiety, and phobias. Low levels of norepinephrine and dopamine have been associated with depression, while high levels have been linked to anxiety, psychosis, and panic attacks. Also, scientists know that certain substances such as alcohol or illicit drugs can increase or decrease levels of neurotransmitters, putting users at risk of mental illness.

What Problems Do Mentally Ill Teenagers Encounter?

Under any circumstances, adolescence can be a difficult stage of life. However, when a teen is suffering from a mental illness, the challenges and obstacles are compounded. Since mental disorders affect so many facets of life—family, school, peer relationships—teens with these illnesses face inordinate problems. Consider, for example, what teens must accomplish to succeed in school. Getting the best grades requires many hours of study, completing assignments on time, and scoring well on exams, all of which can be very stressful for many students. Teens affected by mental disorders are likely to be unable to meet such rigorous demands, since they will usually have difficulties concentrating, staying alert, or even attending classes. In fact, many will drop out of high school altogether. According to one University of California at Davis study, dropout rates ranged from approximately 20 to 30 percent for students with various mental disorders.

> **Teenage mental illnesses are perplexing disorders, since experts cannot determine precisely why some teens suffer from them while others do not.**

Not only do teens with mental disorders suffer, but their family, friends, and others close to them suffer as well. This is particularly true of adolescents afflicted with conduct disorder. This illness is typically marked by a repetitive pattern of disruptive or violent behavior that includes aggression, lying, stealing, truancy, vandalism, and a general pattern of rule breaking. Thus, these actions violate the rights of others. Teens acting in this manner often do not realize how their behavior can affect others, and they show little guilt or remorse about their actions.

Teens Who Harm Themselves

Many teens suffering emotionally are susceptible to physical self-harm by cutting themselves or attempting suicide. Cutting is a practice by some teens who cause bleeding by using a sharp object to cut their wrists, arms, legs, or other body parts. Some teens may even use a lit cigarette or match to burn themselves. According to mental health professionals, teens resort to cutting as a way to cope with the pain of their depression, anxiety, or stress. Some youths claim that they feel a sense of physical relief just after cutting themselves. The desire to cut may even turn into a compulsive behavior that adolescents cannot resist. Many will usually try to hide their cuts and marks from others so that they can repeat the act without being noticed.

A more common way for adolescents to relieve symptoms of their mental disorders or to escape feelings of helplessness is through the use of alcohol or drugs, also known as self-medication. Experts point out that self-medication is merely temporary relief and that alcohol and drugs will actually make mental disorders worse. Furthermore, not only are mentally ill youths prone to substance abuse, but the reverse is also true. Many teens who drink or use drugs are at high risk of later developing a mental disorder.

> **For mentally ill teenagers, getting help from a psychiatrist, psychologist, counselor, or other qualified professional is a crucial first step toward recovery.**

Too often, youths suffering from mental illnesses will resort to the extreme measure of contemplating suicide. According to the Centers for Disease Control and Prevention (CDC), "A nationwide survey of youth in grades 9–12 in public and private schools in the United States (U.S.) found that 15% of students reported seriously considering suicide, 11% reported creating a plan, and 7% reporting trying to take their own life in the 12 months preceding the survey."[5] Suicide is now the third leading cause of death among teenagers.

Can Mental Illness in Teenagers Be Treated?

For mentally ill teenagers, getting help from a psychiatrist, psychologist, counselor, or other qualified professional is a crucial first step toward recovery. Treatment can last from several months to a few years, depending on the severity of a teen's illness. Most treatment includes some form of psychotherapy, or talk therapy. Teens may receive one-on-one therapy, counseling with family members, or counseling in a group setting with other teens. Various types of therapy use different programs to help youths recover. One of the more common forms is cognitive behavioral therapy (CBT), a short-term approach that helps teens develop a set of skills for overcoming their mental illness. These skills include mood

Depression is one of the most common mental illnesses experienced by teenagers. Some depressed teens benefit from doctor-prescribed medications. Those who seek relief in drugs without medical supervision expose themselves to serious mental and physical health risks.

monitoring, increasing pleasant activities, goal setting, problem solving, and promoting positive, realistic counter-thoughts to combat negative thoughts. Teens can then use these tools when dealing with problems or challenges they may face in the future.

Medications to Treat Teens

Adolescents undergoing treatment are often given prescription drugs to help them with symptoms of their depression, anxiety, or other disorder. These medications include stimulants, antidepressants, and mood stabilizers, which can only be prescribed by a physician or psychiatrist. Studies have found a significant increase in prescribed medications for teens since the mid-1990s. For example, a 2009 study published in *Health Affairs* found that prescriptions for psychiatric drugs increased 50 percent among American youths from 1996 to 2006.

Many mental health researchers contend that these medications, while not a cure, can effectively relieve mentally ill teens' symptoms. The National Institute of Mental Health (NIMH) has noted, "Most medications used to treat young people with mental illness are safe and effective,"[6] but that youths taking such drugs should be observed closely for reactions and side effects.

In 2004 the US Food and Drug Administration (FDA) adopted a "black box" warning label—the most serious type of warning—on all antidepressant medications, stating, "In some children and teenagers, treatment with an antidepressant increases suicidal thinking or actions."[7] Many parents and others argue that the safety of psychiatric drugs taken by children has not been adequately studied and that these drugs pose more risks than benefits for youths whose bodies and minds are still not fully mature.

Outlook for the Future

The attention currently devoted to teenage mental illnesses has grown rapidly, with researchers, policy makers, and legislators engaged in efforts to improve the mental health of teens. Many organizations are active in helping teens before behavioral or emotional problems become serious. One method involves voluntary screening of youths in schools and communities, a strategy endorsed by groups such as the American Medical Association and the National Research Council. Many schools nationwide participate in TeenScreen, a school-based voluntary mental health screening program that provides questionnaires to tens of thousands of students each year. These students are then interviewed by a social worker or clinical psychologist in order to identify youths who may be suffering from a mental illness.

In 2010 the American Academy of Pediatrics called for improved training of pediatricians to identify and manage teen mental disorders and issued a comprehensive guide designed to assist doctors. Also, scientists are taking advantage of the latest technologies to make new discoveries regarding the physical makeup of the teenage brain and the potential for mental illness. For example, specialists employ brain imaging techniques such as magnetic resonance imaging scans to study the growth of the adolescent brain as well as the brain activity of teens affected by mental illness. Searching for physical markers in teens' brains, researchers hope to discover early warning signs of these disorders, thus identifying at-risk teens before problems develop. With efforts such as these, it may be possible one day that testing youths for depression, anxiety, and other disorders becomes nearly as common as testing them for physical illnesses.

What Is Teenage Mental Illness?

66 Being a teenager is hard. You're under stress to be liked, do well in school, get along with your family and make big decisions. You can't avoid most of these pressures, and worrying about them is normal. But feeling very sad, hopeless or worthless could be warning signs of a mental health problem. 99

—National Institutes of Health, the US government's medical research agency.

In 2007 Jordan Burnham was a high school senior whose family had recently moved across Pennsylvania to King of Prussia, a suburb of Philadelphia. At his new high school, Burnham participated in the school's news program and was a baseball pitcher as well as captain of the golf team. He was even selected to the homecoming court. Despite his success and popularity, however, the teen felt uneasy and out of place. Most of the school's students were white, and Burnham was often the only African American in his classes. "I think I knew that I had depressed feelings when I first moved to King of Prussia," Burnham recalls. "I felt very alone—certain things felt numb to me. It was difficult to do certain tasks. I felt like I had these weights that were on my shoulder that made it ten times harder for me than for anyone else."[8]

As one of the school's few African American students, Burnham felt enormous pressure to prove himself and excel in academics and sports, and he had hopes of being accepted by an Ivy League university. The teenager seemed to have it all, but hardly anyone outside his family would have suspected that he was actually battling severe depression.

By September 2007 Burnham had already been receiving therapeutic counseling and antidepressant medication. One day, his father discovered empty beer cans and liquor bottles stashed in his son's duffel bag. Burnham became distraught when his parents learned of his drinking. "I'm just a mess-up,"[9] he told his mother. She assured him he was not. However, he then barricaded the door to his bedroom and called his girlfriend. "I'm sorry for letting you down," he told her. "I have to go."[10]

He then climbed out of his ninth-floor window and jumped. Burnham was rushed to the hospital and—amazingly—woke up after a five-day coma with a broken jaw, fractured pelvis, steel rods around his shattered left leg, and a breathing tube from a tracheotomy. A few months later, featured on a CNN television segment, Burnham said, "It was almost like I hit rock bottom. That was as low as I could go. That was as bad as the depression could have got."[11] Today Burnham belongs to a youth outreach group that speaks to students at schools to discuss depression, suicide, and other mental health issues.

Millions of Youths Affected

Mental illness is a term that describes a broad range of behavioral and emotional conditions and is part of the broader term known as *mental impairment*, which includes mental retardation or any physical damage to brain tissue. Mental illness (also known as psychiatric disability) may therefore be defined as a psychological or behavioral pattern that impairs—or interferes with—a person's daily activities such as learning, working, and communicating.

Teenage mental illness affects several million youths in the United States. Approximately 20 percent of teenagers suffer from mental disorders, many of which also affect adults and younger children. Many experts contend that the United States has perhaps the highest rate of teen men-

> " The teenager seemed to have it all, but hardly anyone outside his family would have suspected that he was actually battling severe depression. "

tal illness in the world. According to a NIMH study, "The prevalence of severe emotional and behavior disorders is even higher than the most frequent major physical conditions in adolescence, including asthma or diabetes."[12] These mental disorders can be both disruptive and destructive to many teens, preventing them from functioning effectively in school, at home, or among their peers, but also leading to substance abuse, reckless behavior, and self-harm, including suicide.

Mental disorders can start at any time during adolescence, but actually often begin earlier in childhood. These illnesses often last beyond adolescence well into adult years. As research by sociologist Ronald Kessler of Harvard University Medical School shows, more than half of all cases of adult mental illness begin during the teenage years. Correctly diagnosing mental disorders among teens can often prove especially difficult. Beginning at puberty and continuing throughout the teenage years, adolescent bodies and minds undergo rapid change, and teens' personalities have yet to become fully developed. At this age, kids' moods and emotions can change rapidly, often for no apparent reason. The phrase "typical teen behavior" describes teens who act moody or irrational or who may be upbeat one minute and irritable the next. This type of behavior comes as no surprise to the majority of parents and teachers, many of whom have come to expect it. Whether a youth's demeanor is typical teen behavior or evidence of a mental illness can often be difficult to determine.

Mood Disorders

Mood disorders are one of the primary types of mental illnesses that affect teenagers. These disorders, which affect more than 10 percent of young people ages 9 to 17, include all types of depression as well as bipolar disorder. Depression is perhaps the single most common mental disorder among teens, affecting approximately 2 million to 3 million youths. In fact, some studies have shown depression to be more pervasive among teens than adults. Symptoms frequently go unrecognized in teens because of the similarities to the normal emotional swings that teens go through, or symptoms may even resemble symptoms of a different disorder. A federal study found that in 2007, 8 percent of youths ages 12 to 17 experienced an episode of major depression in the previous year.

Depression takes the form of two main types among teens: major depressive disorder and dysthymia, a milder but longer-lasting form of depression. Symptoms of depression can range from mild to severe. According to the American Psychiatric Association's *Diagnostic and Statistical Manual of Mental Disorders*, major depression exists when five or more of the following symptoms have been present daily for at least two weeks: depressed mood every day; diminished interest or pleasure in activities; significant changes in appetite or weight; daily insomnia; fatigue; lack of concentration, or indecisiveness; overactivity or underactivity; and recurrent thoughts of death. The symptoms of dysthymia are similar, but they may interfere with everyday activities for one to two years or more, according to NIMH, and those with dysthymia may go on to experience one or more episodes of major depression.

> " **Depression is perhaps the single most common mental disorder among teens, affecting approximately 2 million to 3 million youths.** "

Similar to depression, but less common among adolescents, is bipolar disorder. Teenagers with this illness experience severe mood swings, from the lows of depression to the opposite end of the spectrum: mania. In a manic state, teens can be unusually elated, agitated, irritable, or aggressive. They may be talkative or speak rapidly, have increased energy, and be easily distracted. Such teens can also become easily upset or aggressive. As authors David J. Miklowitz and Elizabeth L. George write: "Adolescents with bipolar disorder can become very angry and rage at their parents for hours. . . . Sometimes during these rage attacks, the teen may become threatening or physically abusive toward the parent or a sibling."[13] Teens who are not treated for bipolar disorder are at high risk for substance abuse and suicide.

Anxiety Disorders

While drastic mood swings may be common to adolescence, so too can undue anxiety and stress. Anxiety disorders are illnesses that occur when people are overcome by excessive amounts of worry, nervousness, and stress. According to the American Academy of Pediatrics, "The anxiety may be overwhelming—and at times terrifying—or it may be relatively

> Generalized anxiety disorder is a chronic illness that lasts at least six months and causes excessive worry and anxiety about everyday matters.

mild but incessant, often with no apparent cause."[14] Anxiety disorders comprise a variety of conditions, including generalized anxiety disorder (GAD), obsessive-compulsive disorder (OCD), panic disorder, social anxiety disorder, and PTSD. Collectively, anxiety disorders are the most common of mental health conditions among teens and all age groups, with approximately one in seven youths suffering from an anxiety disorder.

Generalized anxiety disorder is a chronic illness that lasts at least six months and causes excessive worry and anxiety about everyday matters. Teens with this illness—approximately 3 percent, and mainly female—have repeated fears and worries that they are unable to control. In the words of Mental Health America, "They worry about almost everything—school, sports, being on time, even natural disasters. They may be restless, irritable, tense, or easily tired, and they may have trouble concentrating or sleeping."[15]

Obsessive-Compulsive Disorder

A second type of anxiety disorder among teens is OCD, which affects as many as 2 percent of youths. Individuals with this illness have frequent and lasting uncontrollable fears, thoughts, and worries or obsessions that cause severe discomfort. To eliminate these thoughts, along with the anxiety they cause, people with OCD perform routines or rituals called compulsions. One common example is when a teen washes his or her hands repeatedly because of an excessive preoccupation with germs. Or, a youth may feel compelled to do certain tasks in a specific order or to check things over and over again, in order to satisfy a need for perfection or tidiness. In the words of psychologist W. Douglas Tynan, "If something interferes with or blocks the compulsive behavior, the child feels heightened anxiety or fear and can become quite upset and oppositional."[16] Such obsessions and compulsions often consume significant amounts of time, interfering with teens' schoolwork and relationships.

Thirteen-year-old Michelle LeClair was one teen whose life was turned upside down by her OCD preoccupation with germs. She feared that fellow students and objects near her were so contaminated that everything she touched had to be washed with disinfectant wipes. To keep her disorder a secret and to hide her washing, LeClair withdrew from her family and friends. Her need for cleanliness took over nearly all her actions. As LeClair explained: "Nothing was clean enough. I was exhausted trying to keep up the charade. The OCD was creeping further into my brain. . . . My world has shrunken so that all that it includes is OCD and myself. It is so very lonely and depressing."[17] With help from her family and therapist, LeClair was able to battle her OCD and eventually take back control of her life.

Teens with Behavioral Disorders

Behavioral disorders are mental illnesses that affect millions of youths. The most common of these is ADHD. According to Mental Health America, 3 to 5 percent of teenagers—about 2 million—suffer from ADHD, or an average of 1 to 2 students per classroom in America. Although ADHD begins in childhood, the illness often goes unrecognized, so many children are not diagnosed with it until they reach their teens.

ADHD is a condition that affects one's ability to sit still, stay focused, and be organized. Students with ADHD frequently have difficulty following instructions, organizing tasks, or completing assignments; are overactive or fidgety; interrupt others or blurt out answers; and forget or lose their homework. Teens with ADHD have differences in the parts of their brains that control attention and activity. Such adolescents may be impulsive, risk takers, and thrill seekers, and they can often be emotionally immature. To others, these youths may come across as "wired" or "daydreamy." Because symptoms of ADHD may be mild, moderate, severe, or combined with other mental disorders, teens with

> " Teens with oppositional defiant disorder exhibit a persistent defiance and hostility toward parents, teachers, and other adult authority figures. "

ADHD differ in personality, ability to communicate, and intelligence. Although ADHD has nothing to do with intelligence, it has been found that about half of all teens with learning disabilities have this illness. Indeed, NIMH research has found that two-thirds of ADHD teenagers have at least one other coexisting condition such as anxiety, depression, or substance abuse.

Antisocial Behavior and Defiance

Two other behavioral disorders affecting teenagers are characterized by repeated aggression and defiance. Conduct disorder is characterized by a high degree of antisocial behavior. Teenagers with conduct disorder show both a great disregard for the rights of others and a lack of respect for property. This illness consists of four behavior patterns: aggression toward people or animals, destruction of property, deceitfulness or theft, and serious rule violations. Teens may engage in bullying or physical fights, deliberately destroy property, and lie or steal. They may also skip school, stay out all night, or run away from home.

Teens with oppositional defiant disorder exhibit a persistent defiance and hostility toward parents, teachers, and other adult authority figures. They can regularly lose their temper, argue with adults, and use aggressive or obscene language. A teen with this disorder will continue to act defiantly, even knowing that he or she will lose a privilege or otherwise be punished. Oppositional defiant disorder has been called a problem of families, rather than the individual, because of the reaction against rules or limits set by parents or teachers.

Similar to various physical illnesses, mental illnesses are perplexing and unpredictable disorders. Whether mild or severe, lasting a matter of weeks or several years, these mental disorders threaten to disrupt teenagers' daily lives, preventing them from achieving their best during these critical developmental years.

What Is Teenage Mental Illness?

66 Half of all the lifetime cases of mental illness begin by the age of 14 years, which means that mental disorders are chronic diseases of the young. 99

—American Academy of Pediatrics, "Bright Futures: Guidelines for Health Supervision of Infants, Children, and Adolescents," 2008. www.brightfutures.aap.org.

The American Academy of Pediatrics is a national organization of pediatricians.

66 Some of what we see in uncooperative, unresponsive or disengaged adolescents may be early symptoms of a serious mental health problem. It's certainly clear that teens can't pay attention and do their best in class if they're anxious, depressed or caught up in addiction. 99

—Laurie Flynn, "When We're Waiting for 'Superman,' Mental Health Matters," TeenScreen, October 7, 2010. http://blog.teenscreen.org.

Flynn is the executive director of TeenScreen, a Columbia University program that advocates mental health checkups for teens.

* Editor's Note: While the definition of a primary source can be narrowly or broadly defined, for the purposes of Compact Research, a primary source consists of: 1) results of original research presented by an organization or researcher; 2) eyewitness accounts of events, personal experience, or work experience; 3) first-person editorials offering pundits' opinions; 4) government officials presenting political plans and/or policies; 5) representatives of organizations presenting testimony or policy.

66Untreated, depression can lead to devastating consequences for adolescents, including ongoing problems
in school, at home and with friends, the loss of critical
developmental years and increased risk for substance
abuse, involvement with the juvenile justice system
and suicide.99

—National Alliance on Mental Illness, *What Families Need to Know About Adolescent Depression*, 2010. www.nami.org.

The National Alliance on Mental Illness works to improve the lives of individuals and families affected by mental illness.

66Although boys and girls have about the same rate of
major depression during childhood, at age fourteen,
suddenly twice as many girls as boys suffer from major depression.99

—Bev Cobain, *When Nothing Matters Anymore: A Survival Guide for Depressed Teens*. Minneapolis, MN: Free Spirit, 2008.

Cobain is an author and educator on the topics of youth depression and suicide.

66Young people with bipolar disorder may have symptoms more often and switch moods more frequently
than adults with the illness.99

—NIMH, "Bipolar Disorder in Children and Teens," September 23, 2010. www.nimh.nih.gov.

The National Institute of Mental Health is a federal agency devoted to mental illness.

66Research shows that teens with ADHD and learning
disabilities report feeling severely stressed when going to school and sitting in class, feeling tired, having
frequent arguments with close friends, feeling different from other classmates, having low self-esteem, and
feeling that their parents didn't understand them.99

—National Resource Center on AD/HD, "AD/HD and Teens: Information for Teens," 2008. www.help4adhd.org.

The National Resource Center on AD/HD is a national clearinghouse for information on ADHD.

“Teens with borderline personality disorder engage in more extreme behaviors—and more often—than the average teen, and these behaviors impair their social, school and working lives.”

—Alec Miller, “Teen Moodiness or Borderline Personality Disorder?,” *New York Times*, February 25, 2010.
http://consults.blogs.nytimes.com.

Miller is the chief of child and adolescent psychology at Montefiore Medical Center at the Albert Einstein College of Medicine in the Bronx, New York.

“Once considered relatively rare, OCD is now believed to be one of the most common of all psychiatric disorders affecting both children and adults.”

—Daniel A. Geller, “New Advances in the Psychopharmacological Treatment of Obsessive Compulsive Disorder,” American Academy of Child and Adolescent Psychiatry, 2010. www.aacap.org.

Geller is a pediatrician at Massachusetts General Hospital in Boston.

What Is Teenage Mental Illness?

- According to the US surgeon general, 10 million American children—**one in five**—suffer from diagnosable and treatable mental illnesses. This is more than AIDS, leukemia, and diabetes combined.

- NIMH estimates that **50 percent** of all lifetime cases of mental illness begin by the age of 14.

- According to NIMH, nearly half **(45 percent)** of people with any mental disorder meet criteria for having two or more disorders at the same time.

- The US Department of Health and Human Services estimates that **65 percent** of young people who suffer from PTSD are victims of neglect.

- Approximately **1 million** children and adolescents in the United States suffer from OCD, according to the National Alliance on Mental Illness (NAMI).

- As many as **70 percent** of youths in America's juvenile justice system suffer from mental health disorders, according to the National Center for Mental Health and Juvenile Justice.

- Boys are more likely than girls to be diagnosed with **ADHD**, according to the CDC.

Prevalence of Psychiatric Disorders in Teens

A study conducted by the National Institute of Mental Health surveyed more than 10,000 adolescents ages 13 to 18 to determine how severe and widespread mental illnesses were among this age group. The researchers reported that nearly 50 percent of teens had suffered from at least one mental illness by the age of 18.

Diagnosis	Females	Males
Depression	15.9%	7.7%
Bipolar Disorder	3.3%	2.6%
Anxiety (GAD)	3%	1.5%
Social Phobia	11.2%	7%
Specific Phobia	22.1%	16.7%
Panic Disorder	2.6%	2%
PTSD	8%	2.3%
ADHD	4.2%	13%
Oppositional Defiant Disorder	11.3%	13.9%
Conduct Disorder	5.8%	7.9%
Any One Disorder	**51%**	**48.1%**

Source: Kathleen Ries Merikangas et al., "Lifetime Prevalence of Mental Disorders in U.S. Adolescents: Results from the National Comorbidity Survey Replication—Adolescent Supplement (NCS-A)," *Journal of the American Academy of Child and Adolescent Psychiatry*, October 2010.

- According to the American Academy of Child and Adolescent Psychiatry, the prevalence of teenagers with **hyperactivity, impulsiveness, and inattention** is greater in large, disadvantaged, innercity environments.

- Most people with **bipolar disorder** develop the illness in their late teens or early adult years, according to NIMH.

Adolescents Reporting Episodes of Major Depression

Depression is common among adolescents. Data from the National Survey on Drug Use and Health for years 2004–2006 showed that as adolescents (ages 12–17) grew older, more of them reported episodes of major depression.

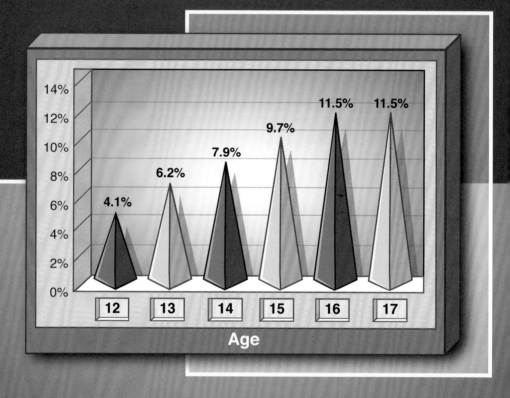

Source: Substance Abuse and Mental Health Services Administration, *The NSDUH Report: Major Depressive Episode Among Youths Aged 12 to 17 in the United States: 2004 to 2006.* May 13, 2008. www.oas.samhsa.gov.

- A teenager's frequent complaints about physical ailments such as headaches or stomachaches may be a sign of **depression**, according to the American Academy of Child and Adolescent Psychiatry.

Age of Onset of Mental Illness

Mental illnesses can begin at many different ages. The National Institute of Mental Health analyzed data for several mental illnesses and determined the median age at which these illnesses began.

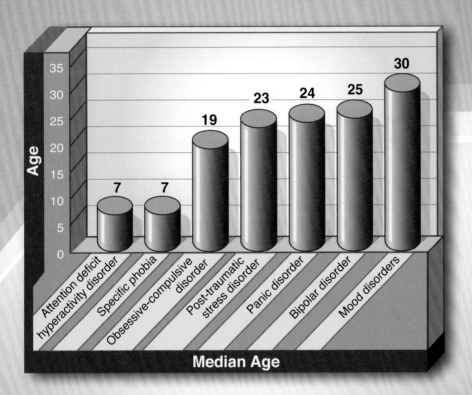

Source: National Institute of Mental Health, "The Numbers Count: Mental Disorders in America," February 11, 2011. www.nimh.nih.gov.

- The symptoms of **social anxiety disorders** are usually noticeable in adolescence, according to Columbia University's Clinic for Anxiety and Related Disorders.

What Causes Mental Illness in Teenagers?

❝There is no one clear cause of mental illness. Rather, it is a result of complex interactions between psychological, biological, genetic, and social factors.❞

—Stan Kutcher, a specialist in adolescent mental health at Dalhousie University in Halifax, Canada.

It is largely a mystery why some teenagers are affected by mental illness while others are not. Some teens' mental disorders begin much earlier in childhood, but others with no previous history of mental problems can suddenly find themselves battling depression, anxiety, bipolar disorder, or other illnesses. The suspected causes of mental illness are numerous and may be likened to pieces of a jigsaw puzzle. Experts know what most of the "pieces" are—perhaps the most important being heredity, as well as stress, traumatic events, exposure to environmental toxins, brain injury, and others. However, no one is exactly sure how all these pieces fit together. As Golda Ginsburg, a child psychologist at Johns Hopkins University School of Medicine, explains: "It's rare that specific events cause an anxiety disorder. There are usually complex reasons why it can happen, and why it can be more intense for some kids than for others."[18]

Most mental health experts agree that heredity plays a crucial role in the development of mental disorders. James Hudziak, director of the University of Vermont's Division of Child and Adolescent Psychiatry, adds: "You can consider that about 60% of the influence on whether a child has a mood disorder is due to genetic factors. This is as high as the genetic influences on disorders such as diabetes or asthma or many of the other complex medical conditions."[19]

Bipolar disorder, depression, and ADHD are some of the disorders thought to have very strong genetic roots. Studies conducted around the world have shown a strong link between heredity and mental illness. These studies have found that many children with a particular mental disorder have at least one parent or close relative with the same illness. Yet merely having or lacking certain genes does not guarantee that a teenager will develop a mental disorder. Consider schizophrenia, a disorder characterized by hallucinations and paranoid thinking. Although this illness has a strong genetic component, studies on identical twins have found that a twin of someone with schizophrenia has a 50 percent chance of not being affected.

> " **Bipolar disorder, depression, and ADHD are some of the disorders thought to have very strong genetic roots.** "

The Family Link to Depression

For decades, scientists have observed that mood and anxiety disorders tend to run in families. Just as parental genes can determine the development of physical illnesses such as asthma, diabetes, and heart disease in offspring, they can also be a factor in mental illnesses in children. Much of the accepted truth regarding heredity and mental illness is based on studies of identical twins. These types of studies are especially useful because identical twins possess exactly the same DNA, or genetic code. For example, when one identical twin becomes depressed, the other will also develop clinical depression approximately 75 percent of the time. Identical twins who are raised separately will both become depressed 67 percent of the time, thus suggesting a strong genetic influence.

The influence of genes on mental illness is clearly demonstrated in a study of three generations of one family. According to the Johns Hopkins Hospital, this particular study, published in the *Archives of General Psychiatry* in 2005, showed:

Children whose parents and grandparents experienced moderate to severe depression are at much greater risk of developing psychiatric problems, such as depression, than those whose parents or grandparents were not affected. In this three-generation study of 161 children, their parents, and their grandparents, nearly 60% of the children whose parents and grandparents both had a history of depression had at least one psychiatric disorder themselves. In particular, anxiety disorders were an early sign of other, more serious psychiatric problems in children from depressed families; the same was true of their parents.[20]

Studies that looked at the rate of depression among adopted children found similar results. Depressive illnesses among adoptive family members had little effect on an adopted child's risk of depression. However, the disorder was three times more common among adopted children whose biological relatives suffered depression.

Other studies have found a correlation between heredity and various other mental illnesses such as bipolar disorder. NIMH reports that when one parent has bipolar disorder, the risk to each child is 15 to 30 percent. When both parents have it, the risk to children increases to 50 to 75 percent. Similarly, according to William T. Goldman, a Texas psychiatrist:

Studies show 50% of patients with Panic Disorder have at least one relative affected with an anxiety disorder. There is a higher chance of an anxiety disorder in the parents, children, and siblings of a person with an anxiety disorder than in the relatives of someone without an anxiety disorder. Twin studies demonstrate varying but important degrees of genetic contribution to the development of anxiety disorders.[21]

A Genetic Link to ADHD

It has been estimated that among teenagers who suffer from ADHD, approximately 30 to 40 percent have another close relative who also has ADHD. In 2010 scientists from Cardiff University reported in the British medical journal the *Lancet* that they had discovered the first direct genetic link to ADHD. The researchers compared strands of DNA from 366 children who had been diagnosed with the disorder to DNA from 1,047 people without the condition. They discovered that 15 percent of the ADHD group had specific segments of DNA either duplicated or missing, compared with 7 percent in the control group.

According to Anita Thapar, a child psychiatrist who led the study: "This is really exciting because it gives us the first direct genetic link to ADHD. Now we can say with confidence that ADHD is a genetic disease and that the brains of children with this condition develop differently to those of other children."[22] The study's researchers pointed out, however, that they had not discovered one specific gene responsible for ADHD. Also, since only 57 of the 366 ADHD children had the gene difference, they reported that much more research was necessary to determine the basis of ADHD.

> " In 2010 scientists from Cardiff University reported in the British medical journal the *Lancet* that they had discovered the first direct genetic link to ADHD. "

Less Sleep, More Stress

Despite the large body of evidence that heredity plays a strong role in the development of mental illness, other factors must also be considered, especially when examining mental disorders among the teenage population. Teenagers today are said to have much busier lives and schedules than teens of previous generations. Demands from schoolwork and after-school activities, as well as teens' preference for personal computers and other electronic devices, seemingly leave little if any free time. The end result from teens cramming so much activity into their day is often inadequate sleep time—known as sleep deprivation—and not surprisingly, an increase in stress. In fact, the American Academy of Pediatrics warned in 2006 that a "hurried and pressured lifestyle" could be detrimental to children's mental health.

Many medical sources advise that most teenagers need about 9 hours of sleep per night in order to function their best while awake. Research has shown that the average amount of sleep for adolescents is approximately 7.5 hours per weeknight, and that 10 percent of teens actually get less than 6 hours of sleep. According to one study of nearly 2,500 Chicago schoolchildren ages 11 to 14, the youths who got the least amount of sleep had lower grades, lower self-esteem, and more depressive symptoms. When adolescents get too little sleep, brain functioning immediately suffers and stress may increase markedly, paving the way for mental illness and other problems.

Unfortunately for those teenagers at risk, sleep deprivation and stress may pose a double threat. Not only can the lack of sleep cause stress, but sleep experts have noted that stress itself can cause significant sleep disorders among youths.

Activity Within the Brain

Whatever the source of mental disorders in teenagers, ongoing research is providing experts with an increasingly clearer picture of what is occurring within the brains of mentally ill teens and how mood, behavior, and brain biochemistry are intricately linked. The brain is the human body's "command center," and all brain activity is dependent on billions of nerve cells called neurons that communicate with each other. This communication is carried out by neurotransmitters—essentially chemical "messengers" made up of amino acids and proteins—that create and control signals in the brain both between and within neurons. These neurotransmitters have a vast influence over complex brain and thought processes.

> " Research has found that when levels of important neurotransmitters are out of balance, mental problems and disorders are almost always inevitable. "

Many times, symptoms of mental illness can be attributed to an improper chemical balance in the brain. Research has found that when levels of important neurotransmitters are out of balance, mental problems and disorders are almost always inevitable. The neurotransmitters most related to mental disorders are dopamine, norepinephrine (also called noradrenaline), serotonin, and gamma-aminobutyric acid. These neurotransmitters operate in parts of the brain that regulate mood, emotions, and behavior, such as sadness, anger, and anxiety. If the levels of these key neurotransmitters are out of balance—either too much or too little—then messages cannot travel through brain pathways properly. This imbalance can alter the way teenagers act and feel, laying the groundwork for an array of emotional disturbances such as ADHD, anxiety, depression, and panic attacks.

> " Advanced technology is allowing researchers to take 'snapshots' of teenagers' developing brains, including the brains of those with mental illnesses. "

The effects of neurotransmitters on people's emotional states are magnified in the case of teenagers. Throughout adolescence, the brain is still growing and maturing. During this time, neurotransmitters are not at their optimal levels, and the pathways taken by neurotransmitters are far from fully developed. In fact, researchers believe that the prefrontal cortex—an area behind the forehead that is crucial to organizing ideas, controlling impulses, and regulating emotion—is not fully developed until the late twenties. Jay Giedd, a neuroscientist at NIMH, describes this complex and fragile environment: "The neural circuitry underlying teen moodiness may not be the same circuitry involved in depression or bipolar disorder. Moving parts get broken. In other words, development may go awry, predisposing adolescents to disorders."[23] Some experts have cited "vulnerability genes" which teenagers may have that, under certain environmental influences, may lead to mental disorders.

Partnership of Genes and Brain Cells

Observers of mental illness among youths have noted an important connection between brain activity and genes. Every human being has about 25,000 genes, and approximately half of those are now thought to have some connection to brain activity, including mental disorders.

According to educational psychologist and author Jane M. Healy, "Certain genes have been associated with tendencies toward stress, depression, or fearfulness on one hand, and impulsivity, aggression, social problems, and risk-taking on the other."[24] Evidence suggests that many different genes may act together and in combination with other factors to cause mental disorders. Of importance are those genes that regulate neurotransmitters. In her book *Different Learners*, Healy writes:

> Brain cells function in tight partnership with their genes. Specialized genes instruct brain cells how to form, grow, and relay the vast number of messages needed for thinking and learning. Meanwhile, outside forces affect these developmental genes in either negative or positive ways. . . . Some disorders (e.g. ADHD, depression) may be influenced by genes that affect neurotransmitter activity in brain synapses, but life experiences also affect the same neurotransmitters.[25]

Scientists have known for years that many different factors can affect neurotransmitter levels. Perhaps most important are substances that tend to be popular among certain groups of teenagers: caffeine in coffee and energy drinks; steroids; and particular substances in tobacco, alcohol, and illegal drugs, to name a few. Once ingested, these substances travel quickly to the brain. Even if teens can manage to avoid such substances, other influences will affect neurotransmitters, such as hormonal changes—which no teenager can avoid—and prolonged periods of stress.

Snapshots of the Brain

Advanced technology is allowing researchers to take "snapshots" of teenagers' developing brains, including the brains of those with mental illnesses. Brain-image scanning tools such as magnetic resonance imaging can take numerous pictures of the brain in rapid succession, thereby detecting brain changes as they occur from moment to moment. Images have revealed that youths and adults who are depressed have lower-than-average rates of activity in their prefrontal cortex. Other scanning results have shown that brain metabolism in adolescents with ADHD is lower in the areas of the brain that control attention, social judgment, and movement.

Discoveries such as these offer hope that scientists may increasingly pinpoint the onset, presence, and severity of mental illnesses in teenagers.

What Causes Mental Illness in Teenagers?

66 Bipolar disorder is thought to be primarily caused by biological factors. It is a disorder that is genetic and strongly inherited, and often begins to manifest in the teenage years. 99

—Gordon Parker and Kerrie Eyers, *Navigating Teenage Depression: A Guide for Parents and Professionals*. New York: Routledge, 2010.

Parker is a psychiatrist and Eyers is a psychologist at the Black Dog Institute in Sydney, Australia.

66 Most experts would agree with me that there is more stress today than in previous generations. Stress triggers depression and mood disorders, so that those who are predisposed to it by their creative wiring or genes are pretty much guaranteed some symptoms of depression at the confusing and difficult time of adolescence. 99

—Therese J. Borchard, "Why Are So Many Teens Depressed?," Psych Central, 2011. http://psychcentral.com.

Borchard is the author of *Beyond Blue: Surviving Depression & Anxiety and Making the Most of Bad Genes*.

"Depression is most likely the result of a chemical imbalance in the brain, which is inherited, or genetic."

—National Alliance for Research on Schizophrenia and Depression, "Childhood Depression," 2010. www.narsad.org.

The National Alliance for Research on Schizophrenia and Depression is an organization that funds research on a variety of mental disorders.

"We know there is a genetic component to anxiety disorders . . . anxious people very often marry other anxious people—a funny principle of psychology—so an anxious child may have a family history of anxiety coming from both sides."

—Harold S. Koplewicz, "Ask a Clinician," Child Mind Institute, 2010. www.childmind.org.

Koplewicz is the president of the Child Mind Institute, a child psychiatric care organization in New York City.

"The developing adolescent brain is very vulnerable to stress and, in emotionally charged situations, teens may overreact. They may push the boundaries and break the rules. They may cry or get angry without apparent reason. As the brain matures, teens will operate more and more from the cortex, where reasoning and judgment occur."

—Linda Burgess Chamberlain, "The Amazing Adolescent Brain: What Every Educator, Youth Serving Professional, and Healthcare Provider Needs to Know," Institute for Safe Families, 2008. www.instituteforsafefamilies.org.

Chamberlain is an epidemiologist in Alaska specializing in domestic violence.

"Biology alone does not explain why anxiety disorders occur. Anxiety disorders probably arise from a combination of additional factors, including environment, development and individual psychology."

—Rebecca Fraser-Thill, "Biological Causes of Anxiety," Livestrong.com, May 9, 2010. www.livestrong.com.

Fraser-Thill is a lecturer in psychology at Bates College in Lewiston, Maine.

> **Unlike neurological disorders, which often involve areas of tissue damage or cell loss, mental disorders have begun to appear more like circuit disorders, with abnormal conduction between brain areas rather than loss of cells.**

—Thomas R. Insel, "Understanding Mental Disorders as Circuit Disorders," Dana Foundation, February 19, 2010. www.dana.org.

Insel is the director of NIMH, the largest federal agency specializing in mental illness.

> **No one thing causes depression, however having a family history of depression, particularly a parent who had depression at an early age, increases the chances that a child or adolescent may develop depression.**

—NARSAD, "Childhood Depression," 2010. www.narsad.org.

The National Alliance for Research on Schizophrenia and Depression (NARSAD) is an organization devoted to mental health research.

> **Researchers [at the University of Chicago and the University of Pittsburgh] found that 18 percent of children diagnosed early with ADHD suffered from depression as adolescents, about 10 times the rate among those without attention deficit disorder. Children with early ADHD were five times as likely to have considered suicide at least once, and twice as likely to have made an attempt.**

—Rick Nauert, "ADHD in Early Years May Up Risk of Depression," Psych Central, October 6, 2010. www.psychcentral.com.

Nauert is a senior news editor for the Psych Central website.

What Causes Mental Illness in Teenagers?

- A 2010 study published in the *Journal of the American Academy of Child and Adolescent Psychiatry* found that approximately **50 percent** of American teenagers met the criteria for a mental disorder.

- According to the University of California at San Francisco, the understanding of childhood and adolescent mental disorders lags **10 to 20 years behind** the understanding of adult mental disorders.

- According to NIMH, **adolescent girls** are more likely than adolescent boys to develop depression.

- Studies have found reduced levels of the brain neurotransmitter **serotonin** in patients with anxiety or depression.

- **Depression** is largely an inherited condition, although a child's past and present experiences and relationships also play an important role.

- The US surgeon general reports that five major neurotransmitters are involved in **anxiety disorders**: gamma-aminobutyric acid, norepinephrine, serotonin, cholecystokinin, and corticotropin-releasing hormone.

Too Little Sleep Linked to Mental Illness

Lack of adequate sleep has been linked to mental health disorders in some teenagers. Health professionals and educators warn that teenagers are not getting adequate amounts of nightly sleep. For many years, studies have shown that the majority of high school students get fewer than 8 hours of sleep each night. Experts contend that adolescents require 8.5 to 9.5 hours of sleep for their health and well-being.

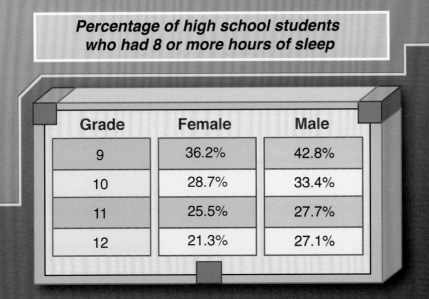

Percentage of high school students who had 8 or more hours of sleep

Grade	Female	Male
9	36.2%	42.8%
10	28.7%	33.4%
11	25.5%	27.7%
12	21.3%	27.1%

Source: Centers for Disease Control, "Youth Risk Behavior Surveillance—United States, 2009," *Morbidity and Mortality Weekly Report*, June 4, 2010. www.cdc.gov.

- Children with a parent or sibling who has **bipolar disorder** are four to six times more likely to develop the illness, compared with children who do not have a family history of bipolar disorder.

- An analysis of more than 50 studies published between 2001 and 2010 identifies a **single gene** that may cause a person to develop depression under stressful circumstances.

Sources of Teenage Stress

Mental health experts have identified stress as a contributing factor that can trigger mood and anxiety disorders in teenagers. Stress has been linked to a variety of mood and behavioral disorders, and teens are particularly at risk from long-term stressful situations related to school, family, and social lives.

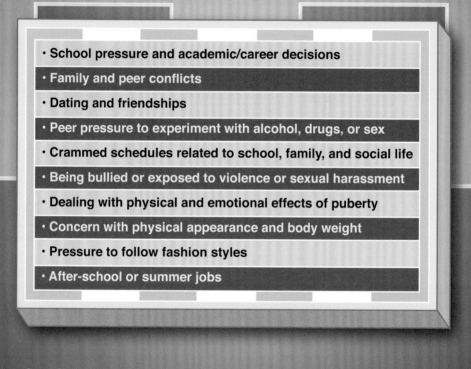

- School pressure and academic/career decisions
- Family and peer conflicts
- Dating and friendships
- Peer pressure to experiment with alcohol, drugs, or sex
- Crammed schedules related to school, family, and social life
- Being bullied or exposed to violence or sexual harassment
- Dealing with physical and emotional effects of puberty
- Concern with physical appearance and body weight
- Pressure to follow fashion styles
- After-school or summer jobs

Source: Clea McNeely and Jayne Blanchard, *The Teen Years Explained: A Guide to Healthy Adolescent Development.* Center for Adolescent Health at Johns Hopkins Bloomberg School of Public Health, 2009.

- According to the American Academy of Child and Adolescent Psychiatry, adolescent anxiety disorders may stem from earlier childhood **separation anxiety**, the tendency to become overwhelmed by fear whenever separated from home or from those to whom the child is attached, usually a parent.

Varying Causes of Teenage Mental Illness

Teenagers may suffer from continuing mental disorders that began earlier in childhood, such as ADHD. Other mental illnesses may begin during adolescence and can be caused by multiple factors.

Lack of sleep: Fewer than eight hours of sleep per night

Biological factors: Changes in levels of neurotransmitters and hormones

Genetics: A teen who has a parent or other family member with a mental illness is more prone to develop a mental disorder.

Poor diet: High sugar, high fats; vitamin/mineral deficiencies

Obesity: Linked to depression, anxiety, and behavioral disorders

Psychological factors: Trauma from physical or emotional abuse; stress

Substance abuse: Abuse of alcohol or drugs can cause depression or emotional disorders.

Environmental factors: Family dysfunction, poverty, divorce, death, neglect

Traumatic brain injury: Traumatic brain injury (TBI) can lead to mental disorders.

Sources: Substance Abuse and Mental Health Services Administration, *The NSDUH Report: Depression and the Initiation of Alcohol and Other Drug Use Among Youths Aged 12–17*, May 3, 2007. www.oas.samhsa.org; National Alliance on Mental Illness, "What Families Need to Know About Adolescent Depression," 2010. www.nami.org.

- Some researchers theorize that adolescent depression may be caused by a malfunction of the hypothalamus, an area of the brain that regulates functions such as **metabolism, body temperature, mood, and behavior.**

What Problems Do Mentally Ill Teenagers Encounter?

66The costs of mental health problems in children are great for our country. They affect children, adolescents, and their families as well as schools, communities, employers, and the nation as a whole.99

—American Psychological Association, a professional organization of psychologists.

L iving with a mental illness can be an anguishing, long-lasting ordeal for teenagers. These youths endure many problems far beyond what other teens typically experience during adolescence. From difficulty concentrating to bouts of serious depression to thoughts of suicide, mentally ill teens face hardships at home, at school, and among peers—often on a daily basis.

When children reach adolescence, their social world expands as they transition to higher grades, enter new schools, and participate in new activities. Most teens have a desire to fit in and be accepted by their peers. But for teens with a mental illness, their condition can cause the opposite—social isolation. Too often, adults and other teens perceive these youths as "weird" or "different" and try to avoid them. These adolescents may be mocked, ridiculed, or shunned entirely by classmates and others. This type of reaction can add to a youth's low self-esteem or feelings of worthlessness. Many individuals who suffer from a mental disorder feel a great deal of stigma. This includes perceiving the mentally ill as unpredictable, incompetent, or even unintelligent. Not only are teens adversely affected by mental illness and by negative stereotypes, but they often avoid treatment, fearing what their family and friends may think of them.

In one of the first studies of its kind, Case Western University researchers studied the effects of social stigma among adolescents aged 11 to 17. They found that 90 percent of the participants reported experiencing some form of stigma, which caused them to feel shame, isolation, a need to withdraw socially, or a need to conceal their illness. As Jean Davidson Meister, president of the Child and Adolescent Bipolar Foundation, explains:

> Parents of children with bipolar disorder discovered the phenomenon of social isolation long ago, and we didn't cause it. Our children are shunned not because we noticed that they are different, but because their peers did. Their diagnoses did not cause the problem, the accompanying behaviors did. Twelve-year-olds are not known for generosity in accepting impulsive, socially awkward classmates. Years ago, a psychologist asked my daughter to respond to statements on a long questionnaire. One of the statements was, "I feel normal." The response choices were "always," "sometimes," or "never." My daughter chose "never." She didn't select this option because I told her she wasn't normal, but because her peers did.[26]

The Case Western researchers found that the school environment can have devastating effects on youths if they feel ostracized by classmates or teachers. Social isolation is considered a primary risk factor for the onset of major depression. Isolation experienced by mentally ill students may increase their levels of anxiety or depression. According to the National Institutes of Health, "Adolescents who have low self-esteem, are highly self-critical, and who feel little sense of control over negative events are particularly at risk to become depressed when they experience stressful events."[27] The combination of social isolation and stigma could spur youths to drop out of school, or worse, to consider suicide.

School Performance Suffers

Mental disorders frequently cause learning problems and difficulties among teens. Depression, anxiety, and other illnesses impair youths' concentration and organization, or cause teens to lose interest in even attending school. The result is often lackluster grades and high dropout rates. According to the American Academy of Child and Adolescent Psychiatry (AACAP):

> Depression usually interferes with a teenager's social and academic functioning. When an adolescent is depressed, school performance usually deteriorates. While depressed, a teenager cannot concentrate. He believes himself to be hopelessly unable to finish schoolwork, and he may skip classes and see his grades drop. Feeling depleted, listless, and incompetent, he may lose interest in extracurricular activities and drop out.[28]

Similarly, teens with ADHD can experience significant problems in their schoolwork. Many ADHD youths suffer from a short attention span, mainly because they are very easily distracted. Other common symptoms of ADHD include disorganization, procrastination, and hyperactivity—or in some cases the opposite: sluggishness. Adolescents experiencing one or more of these symptoms usually have difficulty focusing on and completing tasks. They may misplace homework assignments. Also, children with ADHD can find it quite challenging to sit through lecture-style classes. They tend to daydream, fidget, or talk to classmates instead of listening. Indeed, a University of California at Davis study published in 2010 showed that 32.3 percent of students with ADHD drop out of high school, compared to 15 percent of teens with no psychiatric disorder. This study also found that 31 percent of teens with conduct disorder drop out of school.

Not only are teens adversely affected by mental illness and by negative stereotypes, but they often avoid treatment, fearing what their family and friends may think of them.

The classroom is just one environment where teens with ADHD face problems. In the words of AACAP: "A teen with severe symptoms of ADHD will have problems in all settings: at home, at school, and at play. If ADHD goes unrecognized and untreated, a teenager can develop low self-esteem, frustration, academic underachievement, even failure, and social isolation, which can follow her into adulthood."[29]

Substance Abuse Disorders

Adolescence is a developmental period during which experimental use of drugs and alcohol is common. Research has found that a large number of mentally ill teens also have substance abuse problems. Whether mental illnesses such as anxiety and depression lead to, or are consequences of, substance abuse is not fully known. NAMI estimates that about 50 percent of adolescents treated for mental illness also have substance abuse disorders. This combination of mental illness and substance abuse puts affected youths at a very high risk of impaired daily functioning, causing serious problems at home or at school.

> **Teens with ADHD can experience significant problems in their schoolwork. Many ADHD youths suffer from a short attention span, mainly because they are very easily distracted.**

Some teenagers regularly use drugs or alcohol in order to alleviate symptoms of anxiety, depression, and other disorders. When a teen avoids treatment for mental illness, or treatment is not readily available, he or she may turn to drugs or alcohol in an effort to relax or get relief from painful symptoms. This coping mechanism is known as self-medication. According to Joseph A. Califano, founder of the National Center on Addiction and Substance Abuse at Columbia University:

> Social, developmental, behavioral, and mental health problems hike the risk of substance abuse for teens—and substance abuse in turn can intensify these problems. Adolescents with social anxiety, eating disorders, learn-

ing disabilities, attention deficit/hyperactivity disorder, or depression may struggle more than others to thrive, to excel, and even just to fit in. These teens often use substances to help them cope, self-medicate, or escape the stress of their everyday lives.[30]

Many adolescents begin drinking alcohol in their early teens. Those with mental disorders may be at high risk for binge drinking, which is defined as a heavy consumption of alcohol over a short period of time. According to the National Institute on Alcohol Abuse and Alcoholism, "Children who begin to drink at a very early age (before age 12) often share similar personality characteristics that may make them more likely to start drinking. Young people who are disruptive, hyperactive, and aggressive—often referred to as having conduct problems or being antisocial—as well as those who are depressed, withdrawn, or anxious, may be at greatest risk for alcohol problems."[31] Furthermore, binge-drinking teenagers may be putting themselves at higher risk in adulthood for mood disorders.

Similarly, teens with mental disorders often turn to illicit drugs such as marijuana. According to the 2009 National Survey on Drug Use and Health, 35.7 percent of teens who had major depressive episodes used illicit drugs. Depressed teens are more than twice as likely as nondepressed teens to use marijuana. Studies have also found high rates of marijuana dependence among teens with PTSD or social anxiety disorder.

Teens Who Injure Themselves

Emotional pain is one constant for many teens suffering from mental disorders. Often adolescents engage in a practice known as self-injury: intentionally injuring one's body to cope with a mental illness. Self-injury takes a variety of forms; mainly cutting one's skin with a sharp device or burning or bruising parts of the body.

It can be difficult to understand why teens would injure themselves on purpose. Self-injury is a symptom of emotional distress. It often accompanies a diagnosis of major depression, bipolar disorder, or anxiety disorder. Fifty percent of those who harm themselves report previous physical or sexual abuse. Many youths who self-injure also suffer from eating disorders.

The urge to self-injure can be triggered by strong feelings that a youth is unable to express, such as anguish, grief, or anxiety. Or it may be the result of pent-up anger or a means to relieve extreme tension. Many teens contend that self-injury ends feelings of numbness and that they do it to "feel alive." It is a practice that often becomes habitual, and many teens attempt to conceal the fact that they are hurting themselves. For many youths, a great deal of shame and secrecy goes along with self-injury. According to Focus Adolescent Services, an Internet website focusing on at-risk youths, self-injury is a "coping mechanism, a way to stay alive. People who inflict physical harm on themselves are often doing it in an attempt to maintain psychological integrity—it's a way to keep from killing themselves. They release unbearable feelings and pressures through self-harm, and that eases their urge toward suicide."[32]

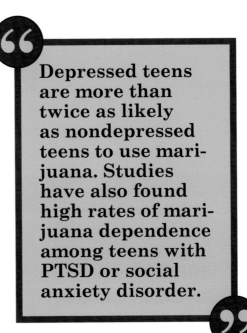

> **Depressed teens are more than twice as likely as nondepressed teens to use marijuana. Studies have also found high rates of marijuana dependence among teens with PTSD or social anxiety disorder.**

Researchers point out that the vast majority of teens who self-injure have no desire to commit suicide. Yet acts of self-injury can easily result in severe bleeding, scarring, or disfigurement. A greater percentage of girls resort to self-injury than boys, studies show. In 2008 a Yale University School of Medicine survey found that 56 percent of girls ages 10 to 14 had engaged in cutting—36 percent within the previous 12 months.

Victims of Suicide

Suicide takes a very high toll on teenagers; the vast majority of those who commit suicide suffer from depression, aggressive or disruptive behavior, or substance abuse. Youth suicides, which number about 4,500 annually, outnumber youth homicides, making it the third leading cause of death for young people ages 15 to 24. Various studies have shown that between 13 and 17 percent of high school students seriously consider suicide. In addition, many attempted suicides go unreported or are reported as accidents.

> A suicidal teen might exhibit a variety of warning signs such as extreme personality changes, withdrawal from family and friends, feelings of worthlessness or guilt, substance abuse, and feelings of sadness or indifference.

NAMI states that more than 90 percent of youth suicide victims have at least one major psychiatric disorder. A suicidal teen might exhibit a variety of warning signs such as extreme personality changes, withdrawal from family and friends, feelings of worthlessness or guilt, substance abuse, and feelings of sadness or indifference. Teens who have made previous suicide attempts— or who talk about death or suicide— should be monitored closely, experts warn. As NAMI writes, "It is a sad fact that while many of those who commit suicide talked about it beforehand, only 33 percent to 50 percent were identified by their doctors as having a mental illness at the time of their death and only 15 percent of suicide victims were in treatment at the time of their death."[33]

It is tragic that troubled children who have lived very short lives would choose not to live at all. Teenagers with thoughts of suicide tend to feel alone and helpless, as do many other adolescents struggling with anxiety, depression, or other disorders. It is important for these youth and the people around them to understand that talking about their illnesses can be an important step toward recovery.

What Problems Do Mentally Ill Teenagers Encounter?

66 Depression and anxiety are debilitating conditions. It's important that parents not dismiss their child's chronic sadness or worry as merely being the result of changing hormones or fatigue. 99

—Susan Stiffelman, *Parenting Without Power Struggles*. Garden City, NY: Morgan James, 2010.

Stiffelman is an author, speaker, and family counselor in California.

66 Being a teenager is hard. You're under stress to be liked, do well in school, get along with your family and make big decisions. You can't avoid most of these pressures, and worrying about them is normal. But feeling very sad, hopeless or worthless could be warning signs of a mental health problem. 99

—National Institutes of Health, "Teen Mental Health," 2011. www.nlm.nih.gov.

The National Institutes of Health is the US government's top medical research center.

* Editor's Note: While the definition of a primary source can be narrowly or broadly defined, for the purposes of Compact Research, a primary source consists of: 1) results of original research presented by an organization or researcher; 2) eyewitness accounts of events, personal experience, or work experience; 3) first-person editorials offering pundits' opinions; 4) government officials presenting political plans and/or policies; 5) representatives of organizations presenting testimony or policy.

66 Sometimes anxiety creates a sense of doom and foreboding that seems to come out of nowhere. It's common for those with an anxiety disorder to not know what's causing the emotions, worries, and sensations they have. **99**

—Nemours Foundation, "Anxiety Disorders," TeensHealth, 2011. www.kidshealth.org.

The Nemours Foundation is a nonprofit organization devoted to children's health.

66 Teens with GAD [generalized anxiety disorder] often have trouble relaxing and tend to anticipate the worst, thus disrupting normal functioning at home and at school. **99**

—New York State Office of Mental Health, "Anxiety Disorders," March 31, 2010. www.omh.state.ny.us.

The New York State Office of Mental Health operates psychiatric centers across the state of New York.

66 During my senior year, I became unable to function. Major depressive disorder shut me down. I couldn't maintain my composure in classes, do my homework, or, eventually, even go to school on a regular basis. **99**

—Jen Wand, "Jen Wand's Story," SAMHSA, 2011. www.whatadifference.samhsa.gov.

Wand is a graduate of Boston University.

66 Teenagers at risk for substance abuse include those with a family history of substance abuse, who have low self-esteem, who feel hopelessly alienated, as if they don't fit in, or who are depressed. **99**

—National Youth Network, "Teen Substance Abuse and Adolescent Substance Abuse Treatment," 2011. www.nationalyouth.com.

The National Youth Network provides educational resources to parents of teens with mental disorders.

❝Most of the time, kids engage in cutting as a way to cope with strong emotions such as sadness and anger, or for attention. It is usually not an actual attempt at suicide.❞

—Steve Sarche, "Ask an Expert: Mental Health Issues Facing Teens Today," EdNews Parent, October 20, 2010. www.ednewsparent.org.

Steve Sarche is an adolescent psychiatrist in Denver, Colorado.

❝For some teenagers, normal developmental changes, when compounded by other events or changes in their families such as divorce or moving to a new community, changes in friendships, difficulties in school, or other losses can be very upsetting and can become overwhelming. Problems may appear too difficult or embarrassing to overcome. For some, suicide may seem like a solution.❞

—University of Chicago Medical Center, "Teen Suicide," 2011. www.uchospitals.edu.

The University of Chicago Medical Center is a health-care provider and research institute.

❝Each year, approximately 149,000 youth between the ages of 10 and 24 receive medical care for self-inflicted injuries at Emergency Departments across the U.S.❞

—CDC, "Suicide Prevention: Youth Suicide," 2009. www.cdc.gov.

The CDC is a federal agency focused on prevention of disease, injury, and disability.

❝One large study on bipolar disorder in children and teens found that more than one-third of study participants made at least one serious suicide attempt.❞

—NIMH, *Bipolar Disorder in Children and Teens: A Parent's Guide*, National Institutes of Health, 2008.

NIMH is a federal agency in Bethesda, Maryland.

What Problems Do Mentally Ill Teenagers Encounter?

- Teens with untreated **ADHD or bipolar disorder** are at risk of having substance abuse problems.

- **Ninety percent** of children who commit suicide have mental disorders.

- Untreated depression is the number one cause of **suicide**, which is the third leading cause of death among teenagers, according to NIMH.

- As many as 4 to 5 times more **teenage boys** commit suicide than teenage girls.

- According to the National Governors Association, US states spend nearly **$1 billion** annually on medical costs associated with attempted or completed suicides by youths up to 20 years of age.

- Teenagers who engage in **cutting or other self-injury** behavior are not necessarily suicidal.

- NAMI states that more than half of young people with a diagnosable mental illness also have a **substance abuse** disorder.

- SAMHSA reports that **28.3 percent** of 12- to 20-year-olds (10.8 million people) are alcohol drinkers.

Effects of Bipolar Disorder in Teens

Bipolar disorder is characterized by symptoms of feeling down (depressed) and high (manic), usually in a fluctuating course. However, the most prominent signs of bipolar disorder in children and adolescents include explosive temper, rapid mood shifts, reckless behavior and aggression. In some cases, these shifts occur within hours or less—for example, a teen may have intense periods of giddiness and silliness, long bouts of crying, and outbursts or explosive anger all in one day.

Depressive episodes	Manic episodes
Sadness or hopelessness	Inflated self-esteem or grandiosity
Decreased interest or pleasure in daily activities	Frantic work activity and increased talkativeness
Anxiety	Aggressive behavior
Suicidal thoughts or behavior	Rapid speech or racing thoughts
Fatigue and loss of energy	Inability to concentrate
Poor performance at work or school	Increased drive to perform or achieve goals

Source: Mayo Clinic, "Bipolar Disorder: Symptoms," January 5, 2010. www.mayoclinic.com.

- Studies show that untreated youth with **anxiety disorders** are at higher risk to perform poorly in school, miss out on important social experiences, and engage in substance abuse.

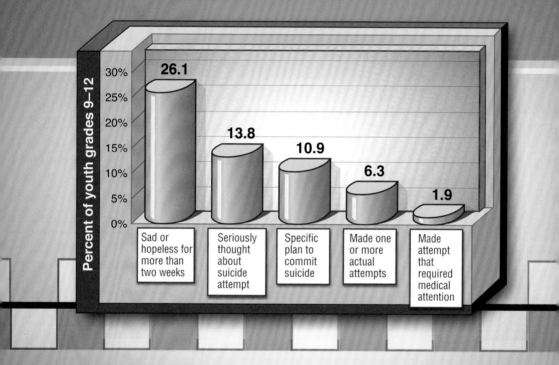

Teenage Depression and Suicide

Many teenagers experience bouts of depression as well as various thoughts related to suicide. The 2009 Youth Risk Behavior Surveillance of more than 10,000 high school students found that nearly 14 percent of adolescents seriously considered suicide, and about 6 percent attempted suicide.

Percent of youth grades 9–12

30%	26.1
25%	
20%	
15%	13.8
10%	10.9
5%	6.3
0%	1.9

Sad or hopeless for more than two weeks | Seriously thought about suicide attempt | Specific plan to commit suicide | Made one or more actual attempts | Made attempt that required medical attention

Source: Centers for Disease Control, "Youth Risk Behavior Surveillance—United States, 2009," Morbidity and Mortality Weekly Report, June 4, 2010. www.cdc.gov.

- One large study on bipolar disorder in children and teens found that more than **one-third** of study participants made at least one serious suicide attempt.

- Research has shown that teenagers with **ADHD** are 10 times more likely to experience disruptive behavior disorders.

Depressed Teens at Risk for Other Problems

A 2010 analysis by the RAND Corporation found that depressed teens were more likely than nondepressed teens to suffer from coexisting emotional and behavioral problems, including anxiety, post-traumatic stress disorder, hyperactivity, drug use, and aggressive behavior.

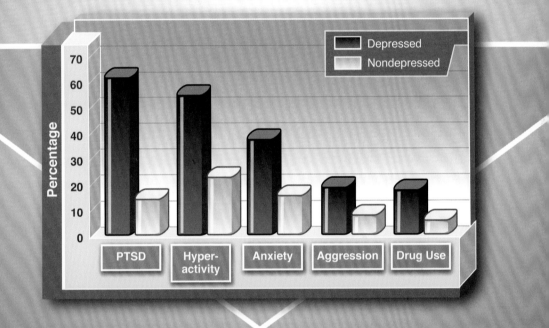

Source: Rand Corporation, "The Teen Depression Awareness Project: Building an Evidence Base for Improving Teen Depression Care," 2010. www.rand.org.

Can Mental Illness in Teenagers Be Treated?

66Help is available for troubled teens through the school counseling or psychology program, community mental health centers, counseling services available through local houses of worship or by speaking to your family doctor in search of private mental health treatment.99

—Allan Schwartz, a licensed clinical social worker and certified psychoanalyst.

Mental health professionals assert that teenagers with mental illnesses require treatment as early as possible and that they risk serious consequences if their disorders are left untreated. However, it has long been known that most teenagers with mental disorders—an estimated 70 percent—do not receive much-needed treatment. For example, according to SAMHSA, fewer than 40 percent of adolescents who experience a major depressive episode receive treatment. There can be many reasons why mentally ill teens do not receive treatment. Some parents and teens may be unwilling to get treatment. Others may not be able to afford health-care costs. Or there may be a lack of treatment providers available.

In order to understand how the treatment process works, it is important to know the roles of various mental health professionals. Individuals with different levels of training are qualified to evaluate, counsel, and treat teens with mental illnesses. Professionals in a school setting will often be the first to notice a youth's mental problems. This could be a teacher, counselor, or school nurse. In other cases a family doctor, pediatrician, or social worker may detect warning signs.

Mental Health Specialists

Teens suspected of having mental health problems may be referred to professionals who often specialize in working with children or teens. Many times, a physician will examine a teen to rule out any physical ailments that may be causing emotional or behavioral problems. With an initial assessment along with a comprehensive psychiatric evaluation, a psychiatrist, psychologist, or other specialist will determine the need for treatment and then determine what type of therapy is best suited for the patient. An important distinction between psychiatrists and psychologists is that only psychiatrists—who are also medical doctors—can prescribe medicine to treat mental illnesses.

Despite the fact that too few mentally ill teenagers receive professional help, many experts contend that success rates are high for youths that do receive treatment with therapy or medication. Therapy, also known as psychotherapy, is the ongoing treatment provided to patients by mental health professionals. Therapy sessions are frequently led by psychologists or psychiatrists, who meet regularly with youths and parents. Depending on the situation, therapy may consist of individual, family, or group counseling. For teenagers, therapy can last from a few weeks to several months or longer. In the words of Mental Health Amer-

> " Professionals in a school setting will often be the first to notice a youth's mental problems. This could be a teacher, counselor, or school nurse. In other cases a family doctor, pediatrician, or social worker may detect warning signs. "

ica, "Therapy can help teens understand why they are depressed and learn how to cope with stressful situations."[34]

Cognitive Behavioral Therapy

Therapy sessions can vary in style and practice. Cognitive behavioral therapy (CBT) is perhaps the most common type of therapy used today. It is a short-term form of psychotherapy that emphasizes the important role of thoughts and perceptions in shaping feelings and behaviors. In the words of bipolar disorder experts Mary Ann McDonnell and Janet Wozniak, this type of therapy helps "identify thoughts that are irrational, distorted, inaccurate, or simply not helpful, and what specifically about those thoughts is causing problems. Next, you work on becoming aware of those thoughts, challenging or rejecting them when they occur, and replacing them with more realistic, useful thoughts."[35] CBT is considered among the most rapid forms of therapy in terms of results obtained. It has been widely studied and has been shown to be effective with or without the additional use of psychiatric medications, as well as having a low relapse rate.

A study published in 2009 in the *Journal of the American Medical Association* found that teenagers ages 13 to 17 who participated in CBT therapy groups were less likely to become depressed than teens who did not take part. In 2008 an independent group of scientists known as the Task Force on Community Preventive Services announced that their review of dozens of studies found that CBT was effective in reducing depressive disorders, anxiety, PTSD, or other trauma symptoms in children and teenagers.

Interpersonal and E-Therapy

Another popular form of therapy is called interpersonal therapy (IPT). Interpersonal therapy—usually conducted in one-on-one settings—focuses on the behaviors and interactions a teenager has with family and friends. The primary goal of this therapy is to improve communication skills and increase self-esteem during a short period of time. It usually lasts three to four months and has been found effective for depression caused by mourning, relationship conflicts, major life events, and social isolation. As the Association for Behavioral and Cognitive Therapies writes, "IPT has been adapted for the treatment of depressed adolescents

. . . to address developmental issues most common to teenagers such as separation from parents, development of romantic relationships, and initial experience with death of a relative or friend."[36]

An alternative to traditional in-person therapy that has grown in popularity is Internet-based therapy, also known as "e-therapy." This approach utilizes the Internet, e-mail, and online chatting between therapist and patient. One such program, called Project CATCH-IT, combines the techniques of CBT and IPT. Project CATCH-IT is a community- and Internet-based program targeting teens and young adults who are at moderate to high risk for depression. The program's goal is to prevent the reoccurrence of depression. The program includes a series of modules that teens can work through privately on a secure website. Each module teaches lessons on topics such as recognizing and reducing negative thoughts. University of Chicago researchers studied 83 participants in Project CATCH-IT and found that the percentage of patients with "clinically significant" depression decreased from about 50 percent at the start of the study to no more than 15 percent at three months' follow-up.

> An alternative to traditional in-person therapy that has grown in popularity is Internet-based therapy, also known as 'e-therapy.' This approach utilizes the Internet, e-mail, and online chatting between therapist and patient.

Psychiatric Medications

In conjunction with therapy, psychiatric medications—also known as psychotropic or psychotherapeutic drugs—are frequently prescribed to treat mentally ill teens. Such medications cannot cure mental illnesses but treat specific symptoms and are designed to help patients feel better and function more effectively. Psychiatric medications comprise antidepressants, antipsychotics, mood stabilizers, antianxiety drugs, and stimulants. All of these drugs affect levels of neurotransmitter brain chemicals, thus causing changes in teens' behavior or perception.

Teens suffering from depression are commonly prescribed antidepressants known as selective serotonin reuptake inhibitors (SSRIs). Serotonin is an essential brain chemical—dubbed the "happiness hormone"—that regulates not only mood, but also appetite, sleep, and body temperature. Serotonin levels are thought to be lower than normal in teens who are depressed. SSRIs such as fluoxetine (Prozac) work to stabilize serotonin levels and are also used to treat anxiety disorders. Fluoxetine has been approved by the FDA to treat pediatric depression as well as OCD. Antidepressants may also be helpful in treating certain phobias, panic attacks, personality disorders, PTSD, and ADHD.

> **Lithium has been approved by the FDA for youths ages 12 to 17, although the way lithium controls bipolar disorder is still not fully known.**

For those teens with bipolar disorder, mood stabilizers are typically prescribed. These drugs are able to even out the mood swings associated with this illness. Perhaps the most common mood stabilizer is lithium, a natural element. Lithium, which counteracts both depression and mania, has been used as a mood stabilizer for more than 50 years. It has a long track record of success in treating adults, but relatively few studies have been conducted on young people. Lithium may also be used with antidepressants to treat some forms of depression, as well as to treat aggression, impulsivity, and substance abuse. Some known risks include kidney and thyroid side effects. Lithium has been approved by the FDA for youths ages 12 to 17, although the way lithium controls bipolar disorder is still not fully known.

Medication for ADHD

One of the most prescribed medications for mentally ill teens include those for the treatment of ADHD. Approximately 2 million teens are thought to have ADHD, and studies show that more than half of youths diagnosed with ADHD receive some form of prescription medication. NIMH statistics show that about 80 percent of children who need ADHD medication still need medication in their teen years. Stimulants such as the brand-name drugs Adderall and Ritalin are frequently prescribed to youths with ADHD to help them concentrate more effectively, and one form of stimulant is even available in skin patch form. Many mental health professionals and organizations praise the effectiveness of ADHD drugs. According to the Nemours Foundation, an organization devoted to children's health, "Most experts agree that ADHD medications are safe and effective when they are used under a psychiatrist's or other doctor's care. And ADHD medications have been shown to help teens with ADHD in all sorts of areas, such as reducing smoking, substance abuse, injuries, and automobile accidents, and helping improve relationships in and out of the home."[37]

Concern About Prescription Medications

In the past two decades, increasing numbers of children and teens have been diagnosed with psychiatric disorders and prescribed medications to help them with their illnesses. According to a Brandeis University study, one of the first to focus on adolescent use of psychiatric drugs, prescriptions for teenagers increased 250 percent between 1994 and 2001. Child and adolescent psychiatrist Scott Shannon warned in 2009, "If current rates persist, within a generation, half of American children will be taking psychiatric medication."[38]

Along with an increase in such prescriptions has come increased scrutiny not only toward the safety of psychiatric drugs, but toward the roles played by pharmaceutical companies and the psychiatric profession in their reliance on medication. In 2004, following reports linking suicidal teens to antidepressant use, the FDA issued a "black box" warning—its strictest type—that required all manufacturers of antidepressants to print clear warnings on their product labels. The FDA action did not ban the use of these drugs, but it declared that antidepressants increased the risk of suicidal thinking and behavior in youths with major depressive disorder and other psychiatric disorders.

> " The FDA issued a 'black box' warning—its strictest type— that required all manufacturers of antidepressants to print clear warnings on their product labels. "

Several years later FDA warnings were also placed on all stimulants, including those made from amphetamines. These warnings recommended caution and careful supervision in prescribing stimulants and indicated that these drugs could potentially cause drug dependence, sudden death in patients with heart problems or heart defects, and new or worse psychiatric problems for patients. Questioning the safety of psychiatric drugs for youths, author Elizabeth E. Root writes:

> Introducing a foreign chemical (Ritalin) into the brain could create havoc in this exquisitely sensitive organ. The result could be one of those undesirable side effects usually mistaken for a worsening of the original condition or the emergence of "an underlying condition" such as bipolar. Typically, the doctor then increases or changes the medication, which further perturbs the brain. . . . The effects of methylphenidate (Ritalin) on the brain are virtually identical to those of cocaine.[39]

Toni Brayer, a physician in Northern California, agrees with Root and others who object to an overreliance on medication, adding: "The sheer number of meds . . . is alarming. Parents and physicians need to question if we are trying to make our children fit a certain mold. . . . I fear the pendulum for using pharmaceutical medications to treat teen angst or teen hyperactivity may have swung way too far. Being a teenager is one big mood disorder. It doesn't need to be medicated away."[40]

Holding On to Hope

The teenage years are well known as a period frequently marked by distress, turbulence, and intense emotions. Even those youths with a clean bill of mental health can experience stress and anxiety from many different sources: pressure from parents to succeed, demands of schoolwork, trying to fit in among social groups, peer pressure to experiment with drugs or alcohol, and much more.

For those teenagers suffering from a mental illness, the path to recovery can be long and difficult. Many kids who suffer from a mental disorder describe daily battles against hopelessness and despair. Yet those who have overcome mental illness offer hope. In the words of author Cait Irwin, who experienced severe depression as a teen: "Give yourself a chance to see how the story of your life is going to turn out. When you've reached the darkest point, you know it can only get better."[41]

Primary Source Quotes*

Can Mental Illness in Teenagers Be Treated?

66 Why is there so much resistance to the idea that a fair number of children—a small and yet not inconsequential percentage—require psychiatric treatment, and medication in particular. 99

—Judith Warner, *We've Got Issues: Children and Parents in the Age of Medication.* New York: Riverhead, 2010.

Warner is an author and a journalist in Washington, DC.

66 There's nothing wrong with getting help with problems that are hard to solve alone. In fact, it's just the opposite. It takes a lot of courage and maturity to look for solutions to problems instead of ignoring or hiding them and allowing them to become worse. If you think that therapy could help you with a problem, ask an adult you trust—like a parent, school counselor, or doctor—to help you find a therapist. 99

—Nemours Foundation, "Going to a Therapist," TeensHealth, September 2010. www.kidshealth.org.

The Nemours Foundation is a pediatric health organization headquartered in Jacksonville, Florida.

* Editor's Note: While the definition of a primary source can be narrowly or broadly defined, for the purposes of Compact Research, a primary source consists of: 1) results of original research presented by an organization or researcher; 2) eyewitness accounts of events, personal experience, or work experience; 3) first-person editorials offering pundits' opinions; 4) government officials presenting political plans and/or policies; 5) representatives of organizations presenting testimony or policy.

❝Once I was diagnosed, I lost several close friends because of the stigma around mental illness. People actually thought that there was no hope, so I began to think that too. It took about six months and then I realized that I wasn't crazy. I realized that I have a mental illness and that I can get better. Even though bipolar disorder doesn't have a cure, I found out that with the right treatment and coping skills, I could be just like everyone else.❞

—Haley Winterberg, "Dealing with Bipolar Disorder & Mental Illness," *azTeen Magazine*, January 2009. www.azteenmagazine.com.

Winterberg is a student in Phoenix, Arizona.

❝The majority of children who take antidepressants will improve with medication. However, combining medication with talk therapy—especially a technique called cognitive behavioral therapy—is likely to be even more effective.❞

—Mayo Clinic, "Antidepressants for Children: Explore the Pros and Cons," November 12, 2010. www.mayoclinic.com.

The Mayo Clinic is a medical practice and research organization headquartered in Rochester, Minnesota.

❝Everyone has seen ads for antidepressants, which may lead you to believe that this is the only form of treatment. It's not. In fact, for teenagers, antidepressants should only be used in severe cases. Often, simply speaking with a therapist, or going to group or family therapy is enough.❞

—Madison Friedman, "Teen Depression and Stress," Stress Free Kids, October 16, 2010. www.stressfreekids.com.

Friedman is a high school student in Rye, New York.

❝About 40 percent of adolescents with depression do not adequately respond to a first treatment course with an antidepressant medication, and clinicians have no solid guidelines on how to choose subsequent treatments for these patients.❞

—Thomas R. Insel, "Teens with Treatment-Resistant Depression More Likely to Get Better with Switch to Combination Therapy," press release, February 26, 2008. www.nimh.nih.gov.

Insel is the director of NIMH in Bethesda, Maryland.

❝When teens feel that they have been part of the decision to enter therapy, and view it as a way of addressing their needs, they are often open to using it to address serious matters of concern, and are usually much better positioned to benefit from the work.❞

—Jonah Green, "Getting Your Teen to Treatment," Child and Family Mental Health, April 12, 2009. http://childandfamilymentalhealth.com.

Green operates a family mental health clinic in Kensington, Maryland.

❝In addition to getting therapy to reduce symptoms of bipolar disorder, children and teens may also benefit from therapies that address problems at school, work, or in the community. Such therapies may target communication skills, problem-solving skills, or skills for school or work. Other programs, such as those provided by social welfare programs or support and advocacy groups, can help as well.❞

—NIMH, "What Treatments Are Available for Children and Teens with Bipolar Disorder?," January 31, 2011. www.nimh.nih.gov.

NIMH is a federal agency devoted to mental illness.

Facts and Illustrations

Can Mental Illness in Teenagers Be Treated?

- There are approximately **7,000 child and adolescent psychiatrists** in the United States.

- The Treatment of Adolescents with Depression Study, funded by NIMH, found that **cognitive behavioral therapy**, when combined with antidepressant medication, was the most effective treatment over the short term for teens with major depression.

- In 2004 the FDA placed its strictest **warning** on the labels of all anti-depressant medications.

- NIMH states that most youths with bipolar disorder will require **long-term** or even **lifelong** medication treatment.

- Side effects from **stimulant medications** such as those used to treat ADHD include decreased appetite, sleep problems, anxiety, irritability, and headaches.

- According to the AACAP, physicians can monitor potential **side effects** from medications by giving teens physical exams and electrocardiograms.

Relapse Rates in Boys and Girls

A study funded by the National Institutes of Health tracked 196 teenagers who were treated for an initial episode of severe depression. The study reported that 96 percent of these adolescents subsequently improved or fully recovered, but 47 percent had one or more subsequent depressive episodes within two to three years. For reasons not clearly understood, girls were more likely to have repeated bouts of depression than boys.

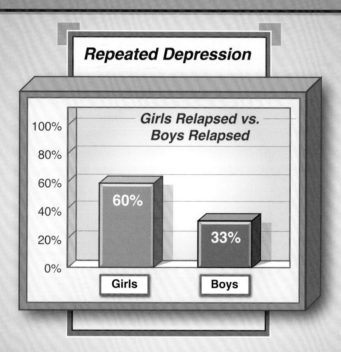

Repeated Depression

Girls Relapsed vs. Boys Relapsed

Source: Johns Hopkins University Children's Center, "One in Two Depressed Teens Prone to Recurrence After Recovery," *The JHU Gazette*, November 8, 2010. http://gazette.jhu.edu.

- A University of Texas Southwestern study of 334 adolescents, who had moderate to severe major depressive disorder, found that more than **one-third** of the teens became symptom free by switching medication or combining a medication change with cognitive behavioral therapy.

Concerns About Antidepressants

Prescribed antidepressant medications have been linked to suicidal behavior in children and adolescents. The signs and symptoms of suicidal thoughts or self-harm may be difficult to notice. These signs are not always obvious, and a young person might not directly admit to having such thoughts. According to the Mayo Clinic, there are warning signs to watch for when a child or teenager is taking antidepressants.

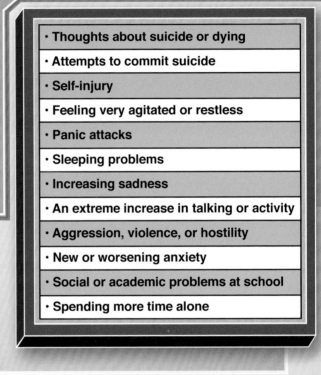

- **Thoughts about suicide or dying**
- **Attempts to commit suicide**
- **Self-injury**
- **Feeling very agitated or restless**
- **Panic attacks**
- **Sleeping problems**
- **Increasing sadness**
- **An extreme increase in talking or activity**
- **Aggression, violence, or hostility**
- **New or worsening anxiety**
- **Social or academic problems at school**
- **Spending more time alone**

Source: Mayo Clinic, "Antidepressants for Children: Explore the Pros and Cons," November 12, 2010. www.mayoclinic.com.

- According to Cincinnati Children's Hospital, it is often necessary to use **three to four** medications to effectively treat a child or adolescent with bipolar disorder.

- An FDA review found that about **4 percent** of children and teens taking SSRI medications experienced suicidal thinking or behavior.

- According to NAMI, when adolescent mental illness and substance abuse are treated together, **suicide attempts** and **psychotic episodes** decrease rapidly.

- **Sudden deaths, strokes, heart attacks,** and **hypertension** have been reported among some adolescents taking ADHD medications.

- According to the Mayo Clinic, **mind-body techniques** used to improve depression in teens include yoga, acupuncture, meditation, and massage therapy.

Key People and Advocacy Groups

American Foundation for Suicide Prevention: With chapters in many states, the New York City–based foundation is dedicated to understanding and preventing suicide through research, education, and advocacy, and to reaching out to people with mental disorders and those impacted by suicide. The organization was formed in 1987, when many of its founders were concerned by an alarming rise in youth suicide.

American Psychiatric Association: The American Psychiatric Association is a national medical specialty organization whose physician members specialize in diagnosis, treatment, prevention, and research of mental illnesses. It is the publisher of the *Diagnostic and Statistical Manual of Mental Disorders*.

Bev Cobain: A registered nurse with certification in psychiatric/mental health nursing, Cobain is a survivor of three family suicides, including that of her cousin Kurt Cobain, lead singer of the rock band Nirvana. The author of *When Nothing Matters Anymore: A Survival Guide for Depressed Teens* and coauthor of *Dying to Be Free: A Healing Guide for Families After a Suicide*, Cobain is also a national speaker and activist for suicide prevention.

Jay Giedd: A neuroscientist at NIMH, Giedd has spearheaded research showing for the first time that there is a wave of growth and change in the adolescent brain. He contends that what teens do during their adolescent years—whether playing sports or playing video games—can affect how their brains develop.

Jed Foundation: The Jed Foundation is a leading organization working to reduce the rate of suicide and the prevalence of emotional distress among college students. Suicide is the second leading cause of death among college students, and untreated mental health problems prevent thousands more students from graduating every year. The foundation was formed in 2000 by Donna and Phil Satow after they lost their son Jed to suicide.

NARSAD: NARSAD, formerly the National Alliance for Research on Schizophrenia and Depression, identifies itself as the world's leading charity dedicated to mental health research. The organization funds research on childhood psychiatric disorders, bipolar disorder, and anxiety disorder. NARSAD invests in new technologies that lead to breakthroughs in understanding causes and improving the treatment of mental illness.

Substance Abuse and Mental Health Services Administration (SAMHSA): SAMHSA is a federal agency that was established in 1992 and directed by Congress to deliver mental health and substance abuse services to the people most in need. Over the years, the agency has operated with the strategy that prevention works, treatment is effective, and people recover from mental illnesses and substance abuse disorders. Its Center for Mental Health Services focuses on the treatment and prevention of mental disorders. SAMHSA funds the National Suicide Prevention Lifeline hotline.

Elizabeth Wurtzel: Wurtzel's autobiography, *Prozac Nation: Young and Depressed in America: A Memoir*, was a 1994 best seller that chronicled her experience with lifelong depression, particularly during college. The book's title refers to the antidepressant drug that was prescribed for her. Wurtzel later wrote *More, Now, Again: A Memoir of Addiction*, an account of her addiction to cocaine and Ritalin, a psychostimulant medication used to treat ADHD and depression. Wurtzel later graduated from Yale Law School and is now an attorney in New York City and a contributor to the *Wall Street Journal*.

Chronology

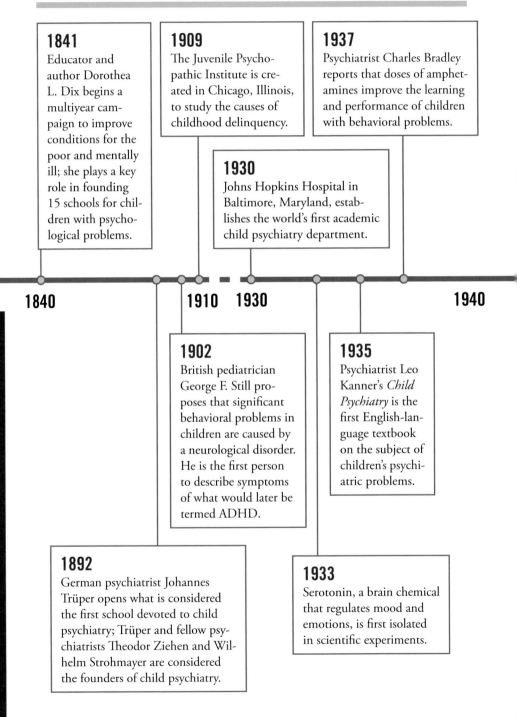

1841
Educator and author Dorothea L. Dix begins a multiyear campaign to improve conditions for the poor and mentally ill; she plays a key role in founding 15 schools for children with psychological problems.

1909
The Juvenile Psychopathic Institute is created in Chicago, Illinois, to study the causes of childhood delinquency.

1937
Psychiatrist Charles Bradley reports that doses of amphetamines improve the learning and performance of children with behavioral problems.

1930
Johns Hopkins Hospital in Baltimore, Maryland, establishes the world's first academic child psychiatry department.

1840   1910 1930   1940

1902
British pediatrician George F. Still proposes that significant behavioral problems in children are caused by a neurological disorder. He is the first person to describe symptoms of what would later be termed ADHD.

1935
Psychiatrist Leo Kanner's *Child Psychiatry* is the first English-language textbook on the subject of children's psychiatric problems.

1892
German psychiatrist Johannes Trüper opens what is considered the first school devoted to child psychiatry; Trüper and fellow psychiatrists Theodor Ziehen and Wilhelm Strohmayer are considered the founders of child psychiatry.

1933
Serotonin, a brain chemical that regulates mood and emotions, is first isolated in scientific experiments.

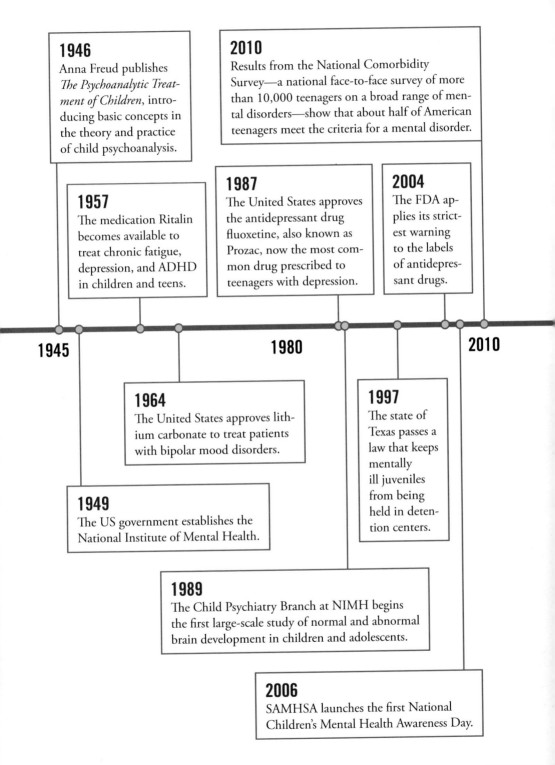

1946
Anna Freud publishes *The Psychoanalytic Treatment of Children*, introducing basic concepts in the theory and practice of child psychoanalysis.

2010
Results from the National Comorbidity Survey—a national face-to-face survey of more than 10,000 teenagers on a broad range of mental disorders—show that about half of American teenagers meet the criteria for a mental disorder.

1957
The medication Ritalin becomes available to treat chronic fatigue, depression, and ADHD in children and teens.

1987
The United States approves the antidepressant drug fluoxetine, also known as Prozac, now the most common drug prescribed to teenagers with depression.

2004
The FDA applies its strictest warning to the labels of antidepressant drugs.

1945

1980

2010

1964
The United States approves lithium carbonate to treat patients with bipolar mood disorders.

1997
The state of Texas passes a law that keeps mentally ill juveniles from being held in detention centers.

1949
The US government establishes the National Institute of Mental Health.

1989
The Child Psychiatry Branch at NIMH begins the first large-scale study of normal and abnormal brain development in children and adolescents.

2006
SAMHSA launches the first National Children's Mental Health Awareness Day.

Related Organizations

American Academy of Child and Adolescent Psychiatry (AACAP)

3615 Wisconsin Ave. NW
Washington, DC 20016
phone: (202) 966-7300 • fax: (202) 966-2891
e-mail: communications@aacap.org • website: www.aacap.org

The AACAP is an organization of child and adolescent psychiatrists and other interested physicians that promotes efforts to prevent mental illnesses and assure proper treatment and access to services for children and adolescents. Its publications include *Facts for Families* fact sheets.

Anxiety Disorders Association of America (ADAA)

8730 Georgia Ave.
Silver Spring, MD 20910
phone: (240) 485-1001 • fax: (240) 485-1035
website: www.adaa.org

The ADAA is a nonprofit organization dedicated to informing the public, health-care professionals, and media about the severity of anxiety disorders. It publishes position papers, the books *Facing Panic: Self-Help for People with Panic Attacks* and *Triumph over Shyness: Conquering Social Anxiety Disorder,* as well as educational brochures that may be downloaded.

Child & Adolescent Bipolar Foundation (CABF)

820 Davis St., Suite 520
Evanston, IL 60201
phone: (847) 492-8519
e-mail: cabf@bpkids.org • website: www.bpkids.org

The CABF is a not-for-profit organization of families raising children and teens affected by depression, bipolar disorder, and other mood disorders. Its website offers podcasts, downloadable MP3 files, and an on-line message forum. Publications include the fact sheets *What Is Bipolar?*, *What Is Depression?*, and *Bipolar Facts.*

Children and Adults with Attention Deficit/Hyperactivity Disorder (CHADD)

8181 Professional Place, Suite 150
Landover, MD 20785
phone: (301) 306-7070 • fax: (301) 306-7090
website: www.chadd.org

CHADD is a parent-led organization with national chapters that provides education, advocacy, and support for children and adults with ADHD. It operates the National Resource Center on AD/HD, which produces the bimonthly online newsletter *NRC News*. Publications include the book *Teenagers with ADD and ADHD: A Guide for Parents and Professionals*.

Mental Health America

2000 N. Beauregard St., 6th Floor
Alexandria, VA 22311
phone: (703) 684-7722; toll free: (800) 969-6642 • fax: (703) 684-5968
website: www.nmha.org

Mental Health America is an organization that addresses the full spectrum of mental illnesses and substance abuse conditions through advocacy, education, research, and service. Its website covers numerous mental disorders that affect children and teenagers. Publications include the brochure *Bipolar & Recovery* and brochures covering depression, stress, and suicide.

National Alliance on Mental Illness (NAMI)

3803 N. Fairfax Dr., Suite 100
Arlington, VA 22203
phone: (703) 524-7600; toll free: (800) 950-6264 • fax: (703) 524-9094
e-mail: info@nami.org • website: www.nami.org

NAMI is an organization dedicated to educating America about mental illness, offering resources to those in need, and insisting that mental illness become a high national priority. Publications include the guide *What Families Need to Know About Adolescent Depression*, the fact sheet *Depression in Children & Adolescents*, and the magazine *NAMI Advocate*.

National Association of School Psychologists (NASP)

4340 East-West Highway, Suite 402
Bethesda, MD 20814
phone: (301) 657-0270; toll free: (866) 331-6277 • fax: (301) 657-0275
e-mail: center@naspweb.org • website: www.nasponline.org

NASP represents school psychology and supports school psychologists to enhance the learning and mental health of all children and youth. Publications include the books *Transforming School Mental Health Services* and *Helping Children at Home and School III: Handouts for Families and Educators*, as well as fact sheets on the topics of suicide and trauma.

National Federation of Families for Children's Mental Health

9605 Medical Center Dr.
Rockville, MD 20850
phone: (240) 403-1901; fax: (240) 403-1909
e-mail: ffcmh@ffcmh.org • website: www.ffcmh.org

The federation is a national family-run organization linking more than 120 chapters and state organizations focused on the issues of children and youth with emotional, behavioral, and mental health needs. Its publications include the book *Transition of Youth and Young Adults with Emotional or Behavioral Difficulties* and the periodic newsletter *Re-Claiming Children*.

National Institute of Mental Health (NIMH)

6001 Executive Blvd.
Bethesda, MD 20892
phone: (301) 443-4513; toll free: (866) 615-6464 • fax: (301) 443-4279
e-mail: nimhinfo@nih.gov • website: www.nimh.nih.gov

An agency of the National Institutes of Health, NIMH is the federal government's chief funding agency for mental health research in America. Its publications include the booklet *Bipolar Disorder in Children and Teens: A Parent's Guide*, brochures on ADHD and other disorders, and fact sheets on a variety of mental illnesses.

Nemours Foundation

10140 Centurion Pkwy.
Jacksonville, FL 32256
phone: (904) 697-4100 • fax: (904) 697-4220
website: http://kidshealth.org

The Nemours Foundation is a nonprofit organization created by philanthropist Alfred I. duPont in 1936 that is devoted to improving the health of children and teenagers. It operates the KidsHealth website, which contains information for teenagers and parents about various mental and physical illnesses. Its articles are available as print-version handouts.

For Further Research

Books

Wes Burgess, *The Bipolar Handbook for Children, Teens, and Families: Real-Life Questions with Up-to-Date Answers*. New York: Avery, 2008.

Michael Greenberg, *Hurry Down Sunshine: A Father's Story of Love and Madness*. New York: Vintage, 2009.

Michael Hollander, *Helping Teens Who Cut: Understanding and Ending Self-Injury*. New York: Guilford, 2008.

Lara Honos-Webb, *The ADHD Workbook for Teens: Activities to Help You Gain Motivation and Confidence*. Oakland, CA: Instant Help, 2011.

Cait Irwin, Dwight L. Evans, and Linda Wasmer Andrews, *Monochrome Days: A First-Hand Account of One Teenager's Experience with Depression*. New York: Oxford University Press, 2007.

Carla Mooney, *Mood Disorders,* San Diago, CA: ReferencePoint, 2011.

Peggy J. Parks, *Self-Injury Disorder,* San Diego, CA: ReferencePoint, 2011.

Frederic G. Reamer and Deborah H. Siegel, *Teens in Crisis: How the Industry Serving Struggling Teens Helps and Hurts Our Kids*. New York: Columbia University Press, 2008.

Lisa M. Schab, *Beyond the Blues: A Workbook to Help Teens Overcome Depression*. Oakland, CA: Instant Help, 2008.

Timothy Sisemore, *Free from OCD: A Workbook for Teens with Obsessive-Compulsive Disorder*. Oakland, CA: New Harbinger, 2010.

Periodicals

Elizabeth Bernstein, "Worried About a Moody Teen?," *Wall Street Journal,* June 29, 2010.

New York Times and Alec Miller, "Teen Moodiness, or Borderline Personality Disorder?," February 25, 2010.

Judith Newman, "Inside the Teenage Brain," *Parade,* November 28, 2010.

Nancy Shute, "Prevent Depression in Teens with Cognitive Behavioral Therapy," *U.S. News & World Report*, June 4, 2009.

Liz Szabo, "Parents: Mental Health Lessons from the Tucson Tragedy," *USA Today*, January 12, 2011.

Ugo Uche, "Telling the Difference Between Moodiness and Depression in Teens," *Psychology Today*, October 20, 2010.

Shankar Vedantam, "The Depression Test," *Washington Post*, May 26, 2009.

Claudia Wallis, "What Makes Teens Tick," *Time*, September 26, 2008.

Eileen Zimmer, "Teen Angst Turns Deadly: Why Girls Are Killing Themselves," *Psychology Today*, January 1, 2009.

Internet Sources

Children's Hospital of Pittsburgh, "Behavior Disorders," February 3, 2008. www.chp.edu/CHP/P02557.

Roxanne Dryden-Edwards, "Obsessive Compulsive Disorder," eMedicine Health, March 9, 2009. www.emedicinehealth.com/obsessive_compulsive_disorder/article_em.htm.

Helpguide, "Bipolar Disorder," www.helpguide.org/topics/bipolar.htm.

Massachusetts General Hospital, "Anxiety (Generalized Anxiety Disorder)," 2010. www2.massgeneral.org/schoolpsychiatry/info_anxiety.asp.

Traci Pedersen, "Teens Disproportionately Affected by Mental Disorders," Psych Central, September 29, 2010. www.psychcentral.com/news/2010/09/29/teens-disproportionately-affected-by-mental-disorders/18922.html.

Public Broadcasting Service, "Cry for Help: Teenage Mental Illness and Suicide," April 2009. www.pbs.org/wnet/cryforhelp.

Robin Reichert, "Depression in Teens and Natural Remedies for Depression," EzineArticles, April 17, 2009. http://ezinearticles.com.

Anita Slomski, "The Teenage Brain," *Proto*, Fall 2010. www.protomag.com.

W. Douglas Tynan, "Anxiety Disorder, Obsessive-Compulsive Disorder," Medscape, January 26, 2010. http://emedicine.medscape.com.

WebMD, "Therapy for Teens: What to Expect," 2007. www.webmd.com/mental-health/features/therapy-for-teens.

Source Notes

Overview

1. Richard Harrington, *Child and Adolescent Psychiatry*. Hoboken, NJ: Wiley-Blackwell, 2002, p. 463.
2. Neil Frude, *Understanding Abnormal Psychology*. Hoboken, NJ: Blackwell, 1998, p. 170.
3. Gayle Zieman, "Panic Disorder in Children and Adolescents," Healthy-Place, December 17, 2008. www.healthyplace.com.
4. American Academy of Pediatrics, "ADHD in Adolescence," Healthy Children, August 11, 2010. www.healthychildren.org.
5. Centers for Disease Control and Prevention, "Youth Suicide," August 4, 2008. www.cdc.gov.
6. National Institute of Mental Health, "Mental Health Medications," 2008. www.nimh.nih.gov.
7. US Food and Drug Administration, "Medication Guide: About Using Antidepressants in Children and Teenagers," January 26, 2005. www.fda.gov.

What Is Teenage Mental Illness?

8. Quoted in Anne Grant, "Teen Suicide Survivor Honored by 'People,'" NBC Philadelphia, June 8, 2010. www.nbcphiladelphia.com.
9. Quoted in Selena Roberts, "A Young Man's Fall to Grace," *Sports Illustrated*, May 17, 2010. http://sportsillustrated.cnn.com.
10. Quoted in Roberts, "A Young Man's Fall to Grace."
11. Quoted in CNN.com, CNN Student News Transcript, February 25, 2008. http://transcripts.cnn.com.
12. Quoted in Kathleen Ries Merikangas et al., "Lifetime Prevalence of Mental Disorders in U.S. Adolescents: Results from the National Comorbidity Survey Replication—Adolescent Supplement (NCS-A)," *Journal of the American Academy of Child and Adolescent Psychiatry*, October 2010, pp. 980-89.
13. David J. Miklowitz and Elizabeth L. George, *The Bipolar Teen: What You Can Do to Help Your Child and Family*. New York: Guilford, 2008, p. 31.
14. American Academy of Pediatrics, "Health Issues: Anxiety Disorders," HealthyChildren.org, August 12, 2010. www.healthychildren.org.
15. Mental Health America, "Anxiety Disorders and Kids," 2010. http://mentalhealthamerica.net.
16. W. Douglas Tynan, "Anxiety Disorder, Obsessive-Compulsive Disorder," January 26, 2010. http://emedicine.medscape.com.
17. Michelle LeClair, "Michelle's Story: Living with OCD," ABC News, August 4, 2009. http://abcnews.go.com.

What Causes Mental Illness in Teenagers?

18. Quoted in Johns Hopkins Health Alerts, "Getting Anxious," Fall 2008. www.johnshopkinshealthalerts.com.
19. James Hudziak, "Dr. James Hudziak on CABF's Flipswitch: The Bipolar and Depression Connection," Child and Adolescent Bipolar Foundation, November 16, 2007. www.bpkids.org.
20. Johns Hopkins Health Alerts, "The Genetics of Depression," August 28, 2006. www.johnshopkinshealthalerts.com.
21. William T. Goldman, "Childhood and Adolescent Anxiety Disorders,"

Keep Kids Healthy, June 28, 2001. www.keepkidshealthy.com.

22. Quoted in Rose Palmer and Chris Chatterton, "ADHD Genetics Is a Complex Issue, Say Experts," *Bio News*, October 4, 2010. www.bio news.org.uk.

23. Jay Giedd, "The Teen Brain: Primed to Learn, Primed to Take Risks," Dana Foundation, February 26, 2009. www.dana.org.

24. Jane M. Healy, *Different Learners: Identifying, Preventing, and Treating Your Child's Learning Problems.* New York: Simon & Schuster, 2010, p. 198.

25. Healy, *Different Learners*, pp. 197–98.

What Problems Do Mentally Ill Teenagers Encounter?

26. Jean Davidson Meister, "The Pain of Social Isolation," Child and Adolescent Bipolar Foundation, June 2010. www.bpkids.org.

27. National Institutes of Health, "Adolescent Depression," December 15, 2010. www.nlm.nih.gov.

28. American Academy of Child and Adolescent Psychiatry, "Your Adolescent—Depressive Disorders," 2010. www.aacap.org.

29. American Academy of Child and Adolescent Psychiatry, "Your Adolescent—Attention Deficit/Hyperactivity Disorder (ADHD)," 2010. www.aacap.org.

30. Joseph A. Califano, *How to Raise a Drug-Free Kid: The Straight Dope for Parents.* New York: Fireside, 2009, p. 110.

31. National Institute on Alcohol Abuse and Alcoholism, "Underage Drinking," *Alcohol Alert*, January 2006. http://pubs.niaaa.nih.gov.

32. Focus Adolescent Services, "What Is Self-Injury?," 2007. www.focusas.com.

33. National Alliance on Mental Illness, "Teen Suicide," 2011. www.nami.org.

Can Mental Illness in Teenagers Be Treated?

34. Mental Health America, "Depression in Teens," 2011. www.nmha.org.

35. Mary Ann McDonnell and Janet Wozniak, *Positive Parenting for Bipolar Kids.* New York: Bantam, 2008, p. 203.

36. Association for Behavioral and Cognitive Therapies, "What Is Interpersonal Therapy?," July 30, 2010. www.abct.org.

37. Nemours Foundation, "ADHD Medications," TeensHealth, December 2009. www.kidshealth.org.

38. Scott Shannon, "Integrative Approaches to Pediatric Mood Disorders," *Alternative Therapies*, September/October 2009. www.wholeness.com/media/Pediatric_Mood_Disorders.pdf.

39. Elizabeth E. Root, *Kids Caught in the Psychiatric Maelstrom.* Westport, CT: Praeger, 2009, pp. 63–64.

40. Toni Brayer, "Overmedicated Teenagers," Better Health, August 15, 2010. www.getbetterhealth.com.

41. Cait Irwin, Dwight L. Evans, and Linda Wasmer Andrews, *Monochrome Days: A Firsthand Account of One Teenager's Experience with Depression.* New York: Oxford University Press, 2007, p. 46.

List of Illustrations

Index

Note: Boldface page numbers indicate illustrations.

Adderall, 68–69
adolescence
  challenges of, 12, 22, 39
  challenges of diagnosing mental disorders in, 24
  stress during, 43
    sources of, **48**
American Academy of Child and Adolescent Psychiatry (AACAP), 33, 82
  on attention deficit hyperactivity disorder, 53
  on depression, 34, 52
  on monitoring of medication side effects, 74
American Academy of Pediatrics, 21, 25–26, 29, 39
American Foundation for Suicide Prevention, 78
American Psychiatric Association, 78
American Psychological Association, 50
antidepressants, 68
  black box warnings on, 74
  combined with talk therapy, 72, 74
  suicidal thinking/behavior and, 69
    warning signs for, **76**
antisocial behavior, 28
anxiety disorders, 13, 25–26, 44, 58
  increased risks associated with, 61
  neurotransmitters associated with, 46
Anxiety Disorders Association of America (ADAA), 82
Archives of General Psychiatry

(journal), 37–38
Association for Behavioral and Cognitive Therapies, 66–67
attention deficit hyperactivity disorder (ADHD), 14, 27–28, 30
  association with disruptive behavior disorders, 62
  effects on school performance, 52–53
  gender differences in, 32
  genetic factors in, 38–39
  medication for, 68–69, 74
    side effects of, 68–69
  prevalence among teens, by gender, **33**
  prevalence of suicidal thoughts/attempts among children with, 45
  results of brain imaging, 42

behavioral disorders, 12, 27, 28
  association with attention deficit hyperactivity disorder, 62
  See also attention deficit hyperactivity disorder
bipolar disorder, 12–13, 25, 30, 43
  age of onset, 33
  effects of depressive/manic episodes in teens, **61**
  genetic factors in, 38
  likelihood of developing, with affected parent/sibling, 47
  prevalence among teens, by gender, **33**
Borchard, Therese J., 43
borderline personality disorder, 31
Bradley, Charles, 80
brain, 16

About the Author

Charles Cozic holds a bachelor's degree in journalism from San Diego State University. He is married with two children and lives in San Diego.